The Russian Tailor of Belfast

Geraldine Connon and Beryl Connon

Clink Street

Published by Clink Street Publishing 2021

Copyright © 2021

First edition.

ISBNs:
978-1-913962-99-9 Paperback
978-1-914498-00-8 Ebook

We dedicate this book to the spirit of all those who made it onto the pages.

Given that they would never have imagined their lives would be laid bare in print, in respect of them you will have to read between the lines if it is scandal, intrigue or indeed any of the vices that you are looking to find.

That is for your own imagination.

Tick tock through time over a hundred years and enjoy a glimpse of how it was.

Well how it was for our extended family, Jewish immigrants who found their home in Belfast, raised their eight children on our streets and faced their own demons head on amongst the spectacularly shameful religious, political and warring divisions on this island and further afield.

Never courting violence or taking sides.

Workers, by God workers, nearly blinded by the hours in their day yet joyously emboldened by everything thrown in the path. Made for challenge.

Even when that joy sunk into despair they coped because blood is thicker than water.

Dare we say they will capture your hearts, they captured ours.

It is their very being, the core of their existence, faith in God that governs our family as it married into Irishmen and women.

We hope you smile with them as they glance back at you from their photographs and we hope you can read what is in their hearts for that fleeting moment they struck a pose in front of the camera.

Dreams and expectations, love and loss, wealth and poverty poignantly all on display.

There was never a struggle to do things their way for their path was their own, a mantle they handed down through the generations.

How could we dedicate this book to just one of them?

Let's just say they all knew how much they were loved.

Yet impossibly we have to name four men who would cast such influence.

Philip, Tommy, Gerry and Danny.

Along with four women, Neska, May, Sissy and Kathleen.

The essence of their lives colour this story and like all the rest of them, none can be done without to complete the picture.

— Geraldine and Beryl

PREFACE

Whom of us ever said these lives we are dealt would be easy?
   Is it all for the taking for those who grasp at dreams?
   This is the story of such people, immigrants who made it happen.

When the timing is right maybe that is the key.
   Add true love to that mix, add children, religion, politics and conflict.
   Nothing extraordinary there, after all, it has been the way of the world
   forever and a day.
   None more so than on the beautiful Island of Ireland or the vast
   Empire of Russia back in the late 1800's, where suspicion and persecution
   equally matched division and man's hatred of his fellow neighbour.

Yet there are those who seem to rise higher from the ashes than others.
   By the Hand of God and for some, a "Matter of Luck".

Philip Leopold was that man, the driving force, the decision maker.
   Rarely is there an opportunity to see inside the privacy of such a family
life.
   Even more rare is their story, recounted by a ninety year old granddaughter,
   written by a great granddaughter and brought to life in precious personal
imagery.

There is no fancy language from the pages, these people could be your own
neighbours
   and you are unaware of them.
   Who they are, who they were, who they belonged to, what they offered
to others and of course what they celebrated, embraced, enjoyed and yes,
suffered.

There is something about spirit in there, a lot about passion for life, work, family and friends ultimately wrapped up in all kinds of love.

Geraldine Connon

"Give me your hand and I will tell you what I see.

Something started with your great grandfather, and is now with you.

Whatever it was I am sure you know.

Tell the story, or it will be gone forever."

Aspirations, now there's the thing. Welcome a touch of that in your DNA and see where it takes you. I suppose you can make them as real as you want them to be and then it begs another question, do inherited skills fall in line with the same premise or are they simply a curiosity? Christianity preaches about the Holy Spirit in us and around us, but sure Christianity does not have the monopoly in faith and then humanity is influenced by challenges from ideology, theology, philosophy, science, anthropology, sociology and some more.

Spirit however, the fundamental measure of being alive, stands unchallenged, virtually indestructible and free to everyone.

There is nothing stronger than the biblical definition, "Breath the spirit which like the wind is invisible, immaterial and powerful."

Who can say that ordinary life is not, in fact, extraordinary?

Who chooses to be the Free Spirit strengthened and emboldened with their secret weapon, the energy of their forefathers?

Who believes in life, in circumstance and in death, the notion of chance is truly a 'matter of luck'? Funny I know some people who do, people who will never forget their roots.

REMEMBER WHO YOU ARE
REMEMBER TO WHOM YOU BELONG

Kriukai, Siauliai, Kovno Gubernia, Lithuania, Ukraine, Western Russia.

30th December 1876 Philip (Preydl) Lepar was born.

In the neighbouring city of Riga Latvia, that same year Rose Patjunsky was born.

The century previous, Imperial Russia under the reign of Catherine II determined that there were Russians and then there were Russian Jews. Laws were passed and a designated area, the Pale of Settlement was created in 1791. Segregation on a large scale as we know it. Purely for religious, political and economic reasons, Jews were not permitted to live elsewhere in the Empire. Except that is for a select few who amongst other things could have been jewellers to the Russian Royal family. Namely Joseph Abramovich Marchak, 'The Cartier of Kiev'.

Kriukai in the middle of the 19th century was home to a Jewish community, self-sufficient both economically and socially yet by no means affluent. It was the countryside, there were those who worked the land and those who carved out their living in the usual trades of the day. Of course livelihoods were won by cobblers, carpenters and fishermen yet economically rural publicans earned more and significantly Jewish tailors held the monopoly over the clothing industry born out of the necessity for specialised religious garments. Those skills and the web of possibilities for all involved would gain form inexplicably out of servitude.

For millennia the growth of flax and the use of homespun cloth was to be Russia's national treasure.

The cloth?

Linen. Mankind's oldest woven fabric, definitive in the role it played in the greatest historical events of the world.

This was the hard trade of the Lepar family.

Ultimately it would be the life and death of them, a few would escape.

THE RAGE OF POWER STRUGGLE

13 March 1881, lives changed in an instant, a simmering racism was to raise Cain as a new hell descended when Alexander II was assassinated and savage rumours escalated throughout the Empire.

Next in line is Tsar Alexander III, a staunch reactionary and anti-Semite, frenetic with power unleashed a fury never before witnessed.

Poisonous unfounded accusations were levied on Jews the critical target even though the revolutionaries of Narodnaya Volya (People's Will) were the guilty party as history records.

The new tsar's escalation of anti-Jewish policies sought to ignite popular antisemitism, portraying Jews as 'Christ Killers' and the oppressors of Slavic and Christian victims.

Consequently a large scale cataclysmic wave of anti-Jewish pogroms swept the Ukraine between 1882-1884 throughout the entire Baltic region and the Pale of Settlement.

The widespread unrest it brought to Russian lives led to the harrowing displacement of 2.6 million ethnic Lithuanians inclusive of hundreds of thousands of Jews who emigrated to the West, England, USA, Canada, Australia and South Africa. The die was cast.

Philip and Rose were born into this climate. Sheltered by their parents.

Leyb and Batya Lepar, along with their family of eight children, were living in the midst of this persecution. As official records show, Leyb happened to own real estate which gave him and his family a greater element of security allowing him to be tax exempt and describing them as 'well to do'. This was a responsibility he took seriously in his community as they followed strict orthodox teachings, education of the faith being the core of their daily life. No family was more sure of their God. So their rural life was good, accepting as tradition dictated, inheritance of land would fall to the eldest son and as the younger sons came of age the law dictated conscription. These were days when Jews were forced to join the army for no less than 25 years, mercilessly even taking children as young as 12. That was Russia, in Ireland land was handed down very much the same way; conscription, now that was a whole different thing.

C'EST LA VIE RUSSE

Not a chance! When boys became men there was unrest in the family, Philip being the youngest knew this was inevitable and coupled with his defiance against the suffocating chains of The Empire he could only see a grim future, maybe no future. He wanted out. He would not be stopped and he would not be silenced. For him it was not revolutionary, it was common sense.

Leyb, the father was staring at a new unthinkable reality, he could see the keen flare in his hardy son.

As conflict crept further into the Pale, it was drawing closer to the Lepar household and with Philip increasingly battling with oppressors, his parents and brothers could see the dangerous clouds circling them.

The Lepar family compound was shaken.

Leyb and Batya Lepar understood survival meant separation, beleaguered and resigned to the prospect, agreed that their unafraid son Philip should abandon Russia. He would not be the first to leave.

Only conjecture could surmise the mood. It must have been sombre and frantic at the same time, emotions would most certainly have been high, after all they knew this day had not been far away. So as Philip and his parents made their way to Riga harbour, for sure by horse and trap over country terrain, hanging onto every minute together, movingly there would never have been enough time between them.

Impossibly they had to let go of each other. Philip, as he saw his opportunity, chose his drawbridge. He was now officially an immigrant.

Surrounded by displaced travellers, his family could only have stared in pathetic silence, for how long remains unknown perhaps for as long as it took night to fall, watching the vessel disappear on the water.

A seabound journey of at least five arduous days and nights with a melee of travellers herded en masse mostly in steerage and at the mercy of chance, no promises or guarantees within reach. Forget about imagining romance, not even in pure brilliant starlight or even sunshine.

THE IMMIGRANT

I understand your fear of me I understand your suspicion
I understand your dismissal You have a life of your own
Would you choose to leave your home, would you choose to leave your
family? I think not, when You have a life of your own
Could you harden your heart to your mother's tears
Could you harden your heart to your father's fears
Can you imagine their pain can you imagine mine
Where lies the future for pity sake
No longer a child it's my life to take
A 'Have Not' I do not plan to be I'm moving onwards, Watch Me

– Geraldine Connon

Philip was barely 17 years of age.

ONE COOL CENTURY LATER
1989 GERALDINE CONNON (GC) STUDIO

STAND BEHIND THAT GRAND WALL YOU'VE BUILT FOR YOURSELF, YOU WILL BE SAFE THERE

"So these are your great-grandparents! Well now that explains it. What a great picture. So you have International blood in you Geraldine, that's what it takes and you have inherited the skills of a tailor! How fortunate, it's in you to be a creator.

I knew my son was going to be a cattle dealer, just like his father. He was never and could never have been anything else", exclaimed Barbara, a loyal client, oblivious to my humour at the amusing comparison.

"Yes that's them on their wedding day, the dust you see inside the frame comes from when it hung over their fireplace a hundred years ago. I'll never clean it."

With a sigh and in my mind thinking, "I'm sure he knew days like this".

As always my attention is drawn back to my client conversation.

"I believe that. It makes sense to me, I can do no other job. Tell me. What do you think about this cloth?"

And so the day continues as every other day does in the studio. Sometime soon I am going to meet myself coming the other way, I have often flippantly quipped. Words that came back to haunt me recently, as I was wheeled into an operating theatre in the Royal Victoria, for an SVT ablation. A problem with the electrodes in the chambers of my heart, which were diagnosed as turning back on themselves, cursing me with blinding palpitations. All like a different life now yet some things stay the same.

Early starts, every minute accounted for and then occasionally when the pressure of deadlines choke me, a sense of uneasiness descends.

It is as if I am not alone. A cool air shivers across my back and whispers past my neck.

That is when the edginess starts, impossible to shake off or stop quick sideway glances with the expectation that someone will be standing there.

Always a moving shadow.

RIGHT, GET OUT OF HERE! That's it, all logic disappears, all machines off in a split second and I'm at the front door by this time frozen and rattled not daring to look back.

Shoulder blades tightened, braced for some imaginary onerous hand to grab me.

What in hell is this? Rearing its head repeatedly in different guises from the Shadows, Noises, Alarm Bells, Strangers in passing conversations. Coincidences.

That endless debate which says there is no such thing. Or maybe it is someone somewhere, telling me, enough for today.

More than often when I glance at my watch, I see that yes, yet again it is 2 am. That is today, that was yesterday too.

Pulling the door behind me, head down, I start the brisk walk home, one of the bonuses of living in a small town. The streets are still and empty. This naivety that there is no danger was foolish as N.Ireland was in the grip of The Troubles back then. The hotspots played it out openly, while in outlying counties nerves and fears quietly simmered behind closed doors. Turning the key, believing it was without a sound makes little difference, be rest assured the parents are waiting, well just mum now.

"Is that you Geraldine? it's very late".

"Yes it's me and yes it's very late and you are still not in bed."

Of course mum is still awake, that is who she is. Family first, then back in the day when dad was unwell, dearly loved and a constant worry, sleep became optional.

Thinking back to when disaster struck the Connon family, an unforgettable Sunday evening.

Gerry, already in ill health having succumbed to a few heart attacks over a ten-year period suffered a debilitating stroke.

This was a cruel blow to a man who enjoyed his work and had one focus, 'family'. He never lost his humour and regained his pride even though he did not make a full recovery. Time was generous to Gerry as he lived for another 17 years allowing him to salvage his 'sweet-tempered' personality.

Gerry Connon and Beryl Rolston fell in love just like many young couples. Theirs was a true romance of the youngest son of a family of seven while Beryl was an only child. The loneliness of being an only child convinced her that would not be her plan. She wanted six children. Gerry for his part had been earmarked for the 'priesthood' not uncommon in his day in Catholic family tradition in Ireland and indeed amongst the Connon connection. Forget it, he had no notion of that for his life, no disrespect intended. He could not wait to leave school, hero worshipping his eldest brother Danny, brothers in arms. Theirs is another long story; two boys from the country, with big ideas.

Danny kicked the move off leaving the home farm in Crebilly, Ballymena for the fast life in Dublin. He had his eyes on being a publican. North or South, whatever and wherever it took to make him a millionaire.

Always looking ahead having worked on his apprenticeship, he then decided it would be the North, Gerry joined him.

They were making strides.

It would be Danny who fell first, that is, fell in love. He may have seen her at Mass or maybe he asked her to dance one night at the Rhinka Ballroom in Islandmagee, anyhow Kathleen Meehan accepted his marriage proposal. To those looking on, it seemed they had it all. Not so.

They were certainly a fiery couple well able for each other becoming proud parents to a daughter, Marie. In their house of very vocal opinions and her father's reckless attempts to lay the law down this child grew up a determined, wilful star in their space who enjoyed defying him. It was a game they played out. Nevertheless she was showered with love and money. There were those looking on saying, there is a young girl who is doing everything from travel to clothes, to holidays, there will be a time when there will be nothing left for her to do. Come the day!

That day came too soon, at the age of 23, Marie was lost to her devoted parents succumbing to a rare cancer two months before she should have graduated from Trinity College Dublin. It made no sense. Nothing was ever the same for them. They would bear that chill.

Gerry and Beryl stood behind them, watching them try to recover. Their young children would attend their older cousin's funeral poignantly following their mother and father's lead to shake their uncle's hand. Years would pass and a new friendship evolved within the extended Connon family. There was a spark of life reignited, Danny and Kathleen became a second set of parents to his brother's youths, enjoying a new stage, treading lightly on unfamiliar ground. Always just in the background. They would enjoy the antics, the struggles and the achievements with none of the responsibilities.

The perfect sounding board.

Danny was somewhat of a genius in business, an eccentric with a photographic memory and most importantly like his brother, he was more than keen on good clothes. Only ever wearing bespoke tailored suits and handmade leather shoes, uppers and soles, essential to his well being as he generated so much static in his body. He was the true definition of a live wire. Unable to wear a watch because of it, improvising by carrying a carriage clock in his pocket. The very good news for me was he was totally enamoured by my chosen career. He and Kathleen embraced and like my parents relished the challenges in the unpredictable World of Fashion.They lived for every moment because I told them it all, their opinion counted. It was new for them, unknown territory but importantly for him it was business. Kathleen and he now had another independent spirit in their space.

Beryl, on the other hand, knew all about tailoring.

She had grown up under her grandfather Philip's watchful eye and as it happened would be surrounded by tailors all of her childhood. When this time of her life had been put to bed who could have predicted what 40 years later would bring. Four generations down the line.

Belfast became the home to Jewish immigrants from the 1840s, the Community growing to around 1,500 at its height in the 1920s through to the 1970s.

Philip Lepar when he boarded the ship in Riga thought he was bound for the USA.

His life took a different turn. When it docked in Hull, England in 1894, this isolated youth would not join another ship, not for that moment anyway. Seems he was in possession of a level of foresight or maybe something more powerful made him stay, anyhow it was all his choice now.

Know thyself. He would pick his direction.

Tinker, Tailor, Soldier, Sailor, Rich Man, Poorman… the choice was Tailor

IN THE BLOOD from 1876

CONNON HOUSEHOLD 1978

This was the best home to belong to. A haven.

Nothing unusual in the grander scheme of things in the early days, then young adults were born. Happy to enjoy their own craziness and differences.

The Troubles in N. Ireland had been raging for ten years. It was unfortunately a Way of Life for my generation. Daily news bulletins of bombs, riots, deaths, road blocks, fighting rhetoric and military presence only halfway through its path of misery became strangely normal.

Astonishingly in the Connon house a bigger fear took hold.

The world stood still and uncertainty weighed the family down.

Illness ever present robbed Gerry of his Freedom of Life.

The dynamic of the Connon family changed, living on a financial knife edge. I had just turned 19 years of age.

My elder brother Brian, my sister Roisin and myself were just heading off to university.

No excuses or get out clauses acceptable.

We had to succeed. The alternative offered a poor future.

Younger brother Michael was following our lead six years later. The baby of the family.

"Some baby"! as Gerry would have said.

Gerry who faced his challenges head on, carried along by love. Only he mattered at that point. Even our doctor would shake his head and call him a miracle man. No one showed a mightier determination to fight for his precious life with his family. That was the battle. Responsibility shifted and the unity tightened. We four young adults on the move had even more purpose.

THE GRASS IS GREENER

As it turned out 40 shades greener.

When Philip Lepar first arrived in England and registered as an immigrant, he joined the enclave of the Jewish Community, extensively living in dismal levels of poverty and hardship endured by swelling numbers of displaced men, women and children. Then out of the clear blue sky in the bleak hopelessness of the English ghettos, a precarious existence, he would not be unforgivingly swallowed up as luck would prevail.

Bespoke tailoring, the largest source of employment, was evolving, the birth of manufacture and mass production had begun and by the turn of the century the UK was the centre of the largest clothing producers in the world. In truth 1901 saw around 60% of all immigrant Jewish men working in tailoring, Philip found his direction; watch, listen and learn.

Hardly a recipient of special treatment it is always about choices.

Thus under the cloak of relative safety within the Jews and with long distance help from his father's connections, his youth in his favour, he moved from Hull to Leeds and secured employment in a tailoring firm manufacturing uniforms for the various government departments. This company as it transpired also secured the contract for uniforms in Ireland. His job? Start at the bottom, a 'gofer', or as the grand title evolved, a message boy. That would have educated him.

This ambitious youth was never going to sit still and so it came to pass that once he had gained enough knowledge of the trade, he was to be shipped to Belfast annually in the spring to take measurements for new uniforms. Highlighting once again naked lack of nerves with a personality in his favour because his English would have been plain scant while at the same time drawing attention to his greatest ability in the trade. The most sacred job in clothes making. The skill of the master pattern-maker, for no matter how pretty the drawings are, nor how good the cloth looks and feels, if the garment does not fit no one will buy it much less wear it. Now his path crossed that of John Arnold, the owner of the tailoring company, John recognised that in him.

By the turn of the cards Philip took up lodgings in a boarding house owned by another Jewish family named Patjunsky, fellow immigrants from Riga in Latvia. They too followed strict Orthodox rules, most importantly for them, 'like meets like'.

This yearly work mission and change of surroundings sat well with him. He could only have witnessed a different type of man and woman.

The Irish as they were at that time and even more so the Northern Irish. A clan unto themselves. It would vitally have been a completely different atmosphere to life in England.

By chance then something else caught his eye, well actually someone else of innate poetic appeal to him. Under the watchful gaze of her parents the innocent young daughter of the Patjunsky's patiently carrying out her daily chores as part of the running of the house was unaware that she had caught the attention of the visiting lodger.

Who knows when he made his intentions clear yet when asked he freely claimed he fell in love with her the first time he saw her. It was the glorious colour of her hair for him.

Remember, to all intents and purposes, he was a lone wolf.

It may have taken him an almighty four years but step by step as he got a hold of himself, the day came and he declared his love for Rose and she for him. He won her and he found her in Belfast, a fellow Russian.

As public records confirm, Philip Lepar made his move and arrived in Belfast in 1898. After four long years in England finally there was someone he wanted to come home to. No doubt he had dallied with damsels, that temptation would have been hard to resist. Now there was an almighty draw, enough to convince him it was time to make his move from nothingness. Ireland would be the door to his life, Rose Patjunsky was waiting for him. She warmed his soul and they saw their future together.

Safely under the roof of his future in-laws, thousands of miles from his homeland, the air he now breathed in somehow felt the same.

John Arnold reached his hand out and warmly shook the hand of this keen young Russian, his new apprentice tailor.

Would he even stay? Would he find his sanctuary? Would he find peace?

Within the year, this unique young couple supported by their Jewish comrades, a modest gathering of the community made their way from their homes over to the first Belfast Synagogue on Great Victoria Street. A match had been made. He had proved himself and so Philip very sure proudly took the hand of his sweet Rose, the year was 1899.

Belfast was on the cusp of the greatest industrial boom in history within the UK through a gradual industrialisation started back in 1798 and despite a history of famine and emigration on the island of Ireland, surprisingly became the fastest growing urban region of the United Kingdom, no other northern cities in England regardless of their similarities matched this boom of prosperity. It was the place to be.

The *Belfast Evening Telegraph*, Nov 1904, records Belfast City as a thriving place, the news-copy laying out advertisements covering Entertainment, Essay Competitions, Church Events, etc, etc. Throwing up many familiar business names. Anderson and McAuley, Brands and Norman, Robinson and Cleaver. Still there was no equality of life.

Let's not remotely view this through rose-tinted glasses as dismally the poor were fiercely poor and the working class enjoyed few luxuries. Although there were many opportunities in most professions and an ever-changing diverse expanding population, nonetheless in sharp contrast, the abject dire poverty of the unskilled working classes living in the slums of the inner city threw up a hopeless existence.

Polar opposites in lifestyle, in beat with the Blight of Ireland, 'Religious Division', reigning forever loudly, socially present whether you were rich or poor and wherever you lived.

As the eighteenth century drew to a close the textile industries of Europe began their rapid and significant move into the industrial era. Although forever the cloth of ancient times linen would now become a global treasure, N. Ireland reigning at the top with enormous profits for many. The first Jewish immigrants of this era from Eastern Europe who settled in Ireland around 1860 brought with them their knowledge of the Linen Industry, namely the families of the Jaffas, Lowenthals and Betzolds, all specifically in the export of the cloth to Europe and in fact worldwide.

Surely their synagogue would have been rife with business deals.

Daniel Jaffa, founder of the Belfast Jewish Community headed up this success story. He was an inspiration not least to his fellow worshippers.

As the century turned within less than ten years, judicious capital investment in technology, principally mechanised spinning wheels would see

Belfast become the epicentre of linen production globally and recognised as a world class industrial city, nicknamed Linenopolis.

Extraordinary ordinary people worked their days out.

Families whose relatives in a previous time had faced devastation from famine to emigration and many years of unemployment all grasped their chances for work.

Salaries were varied, working hours for the working-class extreme.

Trade unions would have to fight their corner.

Nevertheless there was honour in employment.

Belfast would be seen in hindsight as the greatest beneficiary in Ireland of the Act of Union and the Industrial Revolution.

By 1900, it boasted the world's largest dry dock, tobacco factory on York Street, tea machinery, fan-making works and handkerchief factory; even the world's leading soft drinks manufacturer.

All of this economic and social success dismally wed to angry religious and political turmoil fuelled to the point of a civilian uprising. There were arguments for and against supremacy, authoritarianism and nationalism.

The Leopolds were living right in the middle of this, it seems they could live with it. Maybe they could not understand it, too busy with surviving and maybe their attention lay in the new luxury in town of household gas supply for cooking and light, even if it was with a coin in a slot machine.

SINK OR SWIM

One thing is certain their household would gasp in shock with news on the horizon and so the story plays out.

By 1911, approximately 35,000 people were employed in linen manufacture and then visionaries, Harland and Wolff Shipbuilders secured employment for an average of 9000 people, bringing an iconic status to the City, building most of the White Star Lines ocean liners.

A level of employment which has to be recognised, yet with all the promise of possibilities unpredictably just one year later in this air of unquestionable success and a cruel twist of fate, confidence or maybe over confidence, the reputation worldwide of Harland and Wolff would see its notoriety sealed through a tragedy on the North Atlantic Ocean.

15th April 1912 the largest and most luxurious ocean liner ever built, the RMS *Titanic* on its maiden voyage would not live up to its expectation of being unsinkable. As the crow flies at 1246 miles from New York it failed to change course, struck an iceberg and within two and a half hours sank to the bottom of the ocean. In that desperate fight for survival in the early hours of the morning 1517 people lost their lives.

Their hopes and dreams drowned with them.

Northern Ireland awoke to the breaking news headlining the *Belfast Telegraph*, news received from Reuters.

A hushed disbelief descended across the province matched by the atmosphere in the harbour office when in the early hours of the morning they had received the call in stunned silence. First reports suggested loss of life was limited, within 24 hours the full scale of the disaster unfolded. As night fell thousands of people gathered outside the newspaper headquarters on Royal Avenue for news on survivors. The Leopolds this time suffered no losses.

Shipyard workers and employers would, 18 employees, eight men who worked on the build, one who died during the launch and nine who sailed on the maiden voyage.

The reputation of the yard was at stake as it sat on pressing orders amounting to the construction of 17 new ships. Work had to proceed. There was no time for remorse or sympathy, no work, no pay at all levels leaving extended families, friends and work colleagues to mind their own losses. Back then it seemed understanding grief was short in measure.

We can only reflect on the despondency that would have been in the air.

Dip your hands in water and as the ripples calm, it is as if nothing happened. Back in 1912, the talk would settle, people carried on.

This was and is the capacity of the Northern Irish, other things to deal with, other things to worry about, counting your blessings.

Pointedly, apart from the religious division, segregation had another arrow as financial security and wealth were the other immense divisions in Belfast City. The rich lived mostly on the south side in large architecturally beautiful houses on tree-lined avenues, parades and parks, while the poor lived in crowded red brick terraced houses, only just surviving.

Philip and Rose had to start somewhere, that would make their rise even more momentous. As he continued to make waves in the rag trade, gaining a foothold in the workplace they would join the red brick throng moving from small houses to houses, each with its own memories.

Amongst thousands of other working class grinders they lived in these postage stamp sized dwellings, houses full of very poor people in wretched poverty. However this couple were not standing still. They would move house no less than five times to find their peace.

Lodgings for them are recorded at Bristol Street when they first married until 1901, then to Newport Street. It would most definitely have been a poor existence. Two years later they lodged on Roe Street, near Manor Street at some point in 1904, and as his skills and work status improved, work took them to the vicinity of the Antrim Road and a home at Salisbury Avenue. They were gaining ground.

This suburb of the City became N. Ireland's Jewish Settlement. They were also gaining numbers, with their boundless energy.

This raw passion as it turns out, undeniable, as laid out by the 1911 census. Rose registered herself as a housekeeper and mother of six children.

They were, after all, orthodox.

For anyone who adds a soul to the Jewish people is considered as if he built an entire world. They were fulfilling the bare biblical law of the obligation to procreate. For them not a hardship, a love pact. Energised by their children, these foreigners were surviving in all matters of life. Interestingly, not yet still speaking and certainly unable to write any clear English. The fully fledged young lady and now mother wistfully made her

mark on the official document with an ✗

Philip had held onto his family name Lepar while in England. Then following advice he had a choice to make. Looking to Europe he decided that Philip Lepar should legally become Philip Leopold. He would be fit to sign his name on the document.

THE LEOPOLD KINDER OF THE EARLY 1900S

The Leopolds within a year and a half of their marriage welcomed their first daughter into their lives. By their tenth anniversary they had seven girls. Seems that Rose caught her breath for five years and then gave birth to two more babies.

Bea 1901, Dolly 1902, Edith 1904, Peggy 1906, Millie (Minka) 1907, Nettie (Neska) 1909, Samuel (Sonny) 1915, Lillian (Lallie) 1917.

Sadly the fourth child Rebecca born 9th December 1905 seems to have been a cause for great worry. No photograph can be found of her. Her very existence only coming to light on the 1911 Census and then she just disappears, to us anyway. Maybe the births were all too close together for her mother and her health was showing the first signs of weakness. Would 'Trojans' best describe these parents?

The family hence established themselves fully into the spirit of their neck of the woods. Communicating via gestures with their neighbours.

These Russians with their N. Irish brood were a familiar sight around Cavehill and the surrounding area.

Always dressed impeccably, never more so than on the days their proud parents waltzed them into the local photographer's studio to have their portraits captured.

A familiar and frequent outing which their father so joyously embraced at the drop of a hat.

In fact sitting for a portrait would become his most favoured pastime and lifelong pleasure.

As parents and worse still as Jewish parents, did they fuss over their girls. They had made their home in Belfast with no plans to leave, taken that huge leap of faith and were gathering purpose. It would become a house full of chat and opinion, no wilting lilies.

The girls were the centre of attention, raised as Jews, but the Irishness was creeping in.

Typically they understood Yiddish but as they mixed with the locals and made friends they would soon come to learn English attending Clifton Primary School. Then in 1907 the highly respected Jaffa family synonymous with the Jewish congregation continued to do what they did best, show leadership. Well before their time they built the Jaffa primary school welcoming all denominations, applauding the merits of integration. Some not so young would take advantage of the teaching, maybe not officially, how else did Philip Leopold learn how to sign his name? He was friendly with the headmaster of course. How would he ever conduct business without his signature?

A LITTLE INFORMATION IS A DANGEROUS THING

As for the Jaffas, they wielded great influence in the synagogue.

Their vision under the guidance of the now patriarch Otto Jaffa, son of Daniel, was wide ranging in Irish society, from substantial economic success in business, the largest exporter of linen in Ireland and solid employers of up to 650 people by 1914 when the company expanded to making munitions and most significantly Otto's determination directed at the importance of education. His contributions on several committees such as the Irish Technical Education Board led to the establishment of Queen's University and secured the Public Libraries Act extended to Belfast leading to the establishment of the first free library in the city.

As if the norm, Otto would continue to excel in civic duty, welcomed and elected as a Justice of the Peace, a governor of the Royal Hospital and the German Consul in Belfast, he would find himself elected Lord Mayor of the city in 1899 and again in 1904.

In 1900 he was knighted at Dublin Castle and the following year he reigned as High Sheriff of Belfast. Ultimately, a man who attained huge successes, possessive of the Midas touch.

Yet, they were caught up in a travesty of justice as a volatile turn of loyalty showed that in spite of all his work, business foresight and total commitment to N. Ireland, public support is more than fragile, never a necessary given, as the Jaffas saw their lives swiftly pulled asunder.

After the outbreak of WWI, anti-German feelings gathered speed.

Otto Jaffa would certainly have been very conscious of the developing crisis, taking solace of sorts, in the fact that he had been naturalised as a British citizen and denaturalized as a German as far back as 1880.

Beyond that he was very well known in Unionist circles, it all made no sense even more so despite his loyalty to the Crown and his eldest son Arthur and his nephew serving in the British Army.

Disquietingly, the Jaffas could see their very existence was being grossly undermined, as they attempted to carry on as much as normality would allow, and maybe would have held onto their hard-earned high position in society life in Ireland but for the carnage of war close to this island.

World news coverage reports, on the 7th of May 1915 as the war moved into its sixth month, the Germans targeted and torpedoed a civilian cruise liner, the *Lusitania* heading for Liverpool off the coast of Cork. Over a 1000 people drowned. Now, anti-German feelings in the United Kingdom rose to fever pitch. Riots broke out in major cities nationwide and German businesses were attacked and homes destroyed. Government advice was for all Germans to apply for places in internment camps for their own safety. That atmosphere was made all the worse by lamentable news coverage of the bodies of the victims being carried ashore from the wreckage.

Otto and his family faced devastation as these attacks became personal, after 25 years of irreproachable service and most generous philanthropy.

Highlighting the adage that a little knowledge is a very dangerous thing.

Sir Otto answered newspaper protests by writing to the Northern Whig, a letter which they printed on May the 18th 1915. He laid bare the depth of his feelings publicly, a man overwhelmed with pain and sorrow.

Otto closed the doors to his beloved home Kin Edar. All too late for shattered confidences and relationships, Otto's choice was to maintain his dignity, leading him to resign his post as Alderman of Windsor Ward from Belfast City Council in June 1916 as he approached 70 years of age. The members of Council, for their part, expressed deep regret at the circumstances which had led to his resignation.

His Jewish roots were not considered at this time, his German heritage would damn him. A shameful, poor reward for such a gentleman. He and his wife would leave Belfast for London, never to return.

The Congregation of the Belfast synagogue would see it differently as they continued to flourish from Jaffa's influence and support.

The Community continued to expand in the immediate years and through their desire for freedom from persecution and their capacity for work they made themselves an integral part of their neighbours' lives. Establishing small businesses, delicatessens, fruit shops, butchers, tailors, money lenders, jewellers, schools, law, medicine and the arts.

'Little Russia' in North Belfast, never a threat, either to Catholic or Protestant. Their religion for the first time was in their favour. The culture of Ireland was not merciless to Judaism. That was a fine thing.

Unfortunately not enough to save Otto Jaffa as he faithfully worshipped amongst them loving his fellow man, his native ancestry failed him.

Rabbi Shachter, religious head of the Jewish Community at this time, knew him well and would pay him a befitting tribute in the Belfast Newsletter upon his death 13 years later, describing him as he was; a noble child of a noble family whose single-hearted love of humanity gained for him affection and reverence of all classes and creeds.

Certainly the Leopolds were gracious of the opportunities in front of them. Philip was inspired by his peers, Otto Jaffa was one of them.

As his family was growing, home and work life were good, offering the promise of betterment. When Philip and Rose looked at each other they had an inbuilt understanding of when to speak and when to keep quiet. They thought the same way and behaved that way privately and in public, mostly speaking in Yiddish. Whom among us does not understand the value of keeping schtum.

So from 1901 until 1915 the six Leopold girls enjoyed the autonomy of the home, constantly vying for Dada's attention and were really excited to welcome their new sister to the party as their gracious mother was pregnant again. This was her seventh home birth, stoic Rose showed wicked strength, be that as it may, living out the pact of their marriage.

Then hell froze over, a big boy was born, Samuel made an appearance and he was to take centre stage. The limelight was his to steal.

Flickers of possessiveness appeared, was he going to capture all of Dada's love and affection? Not at all, that would never happen.

Philip by now had opened his draper's shop on the Old Park Road while continuing to learn the tailoring trade. So is it an opportunity or an educated gamble? It certainly was hard earned, he would have worked from when he got up in the morning until the day was over at whatever time that ended up, knowing he had happiness and humour awaiting him at home. A terraced abode of seven children at this stage, some new drama or childish chatter you could be sure of. Now the girls found a new rival amongst them, they could not miss but witness their mother and father's elation, a son for them. What was this all about? They did not ask for a brother and neither did they need one.

Surely he could not be the favourite? No one became more unhinged than Neska, she needed sweetening. She had enjoyed her role as baby.

Every night when Dada got home from work for weeks on end, he had to habitually waltz his youngest daughter on his shoulders throughout the house to win her round to the new arrival. Neska, all of six years old, lamented that maybe the best thing to do was to flush him down the toilet. After all she had been the baby of the family and now all eyes were on a boy. This baby girl was not happy!

Philip could barely contain his excitement and pride now that he had a son, still the girls were everything, his youngest daughter his living image. There was a new edge to competition in the house softened slightly by the arrival of yet another girl. The seventh living daughter named Lallie completed the Leopolds. If she had been a boy the parents would have assumed the mould was broken and they would have kept going to have more boys. A blessing in disguise then for Rose, eight children living one dead, Enough!

According to Jewish law Philip's Hebrew name would become Predyl Yomtov ben David. Now, he had a son who would say Kaddish for him. That role was saved only for a son. The Russian-Irish were fulfilled.

By the first light of the following day, chest swollen with pride, there he stood outside his shop directing the sign writer as he repainted the Title of the premises to 'Philip Leopold and Son'.

Such were his expectations of the mantle he envisaged handing down. Having hit the ground running when he looked back, now he could see progress. The socialiser emerged.

Of course he was always deep in the center of whatever was happening, amongst the children, in the synagogue, with his friends and in work. That was him.

So trivial as it may read today Philip thought the same. That long running question of who makes the rules and the sparsity of commonsense which floated in the air then too.

Bow to the lawmakers who never kept a business afloat!

Alot did, some did not. Take your chances if you will.

Nevertheless, the following couple of editorials give an essence of and lay bare the draconian times. When your livelihood is in a savage business, who counts the working hours?

Keeping the sabbath!

BELFAST 1907–15 TRADING IN OLD FASHIONED TIMES
THE LAY OF THE LAND & THE LAW OF THE LAND

JUST FOR THE RECORD

A trait humorous to his Northern Irish friends and neighbours, maybe not so to the judiciary regime. Philip blissfully created his own heaven around him, seemingly only slightly interested in the law.

"Vot vos he talking about? Or vot did he say?" was frequently his response whatever the crime or folly, for him it was all about survival for the workers, it was not murder it was empathy.

He would have his days in court.

1907 June18, LAW COURTS BELFAST

I do wonder and can see a vision of him impeccably turned out, standing in the dock nodding in agreement but not really fazed, not because he did not understand the charge, more so that he would have been watching his time pondering deadlines to be met.

Newspaper coverage of the judicial service of that time, portrays and reports it perfectly in its stilted palaver, inveterate legal jargon difficult at the best of times, but the crimes! No wonder it was tempting to plead ignorance.

So on this occasion the newsletter copy describes the illegality as a curious series of prosecutions, under the Factory and Workshop Acts 1901.

This would surely be a test for Philip and his employer.

Mr W. Williams, H.M Inspector of Factories, summoned Messrs, J. N. & R. Arnold, Tailors, 61 Upper Library Street, for having on 31st May employed Annie Dolaghan and four other women otherwise than in accordance with the period of employment specified in the notice in the workshop. Mr Wm. Tughan represented the defendants who in turn prosecuted their foreman, Philip Leopold, for having employed the women without their consent, knowledge or connivance.

Mr Williams gave evidence as to his assistant discovering the women working before 8 am. It was stated by the foreman at the time that his employers were not aware that the workers were in so early.

Mr Tughan, prosecuting for the firm against the foreman, said the man had been given special directions not to employ the women outside specific hours. It seemed that on the day in question they desired to go to an entertainment and agreed to come in early if they got out before the usual time and without the knowledge of Mr Arnold, Leopold consented to this.

After discussion.

The case against Messrs. Arnold for the employment of Annie Dolaghan was dismissed and the summonses against the other women were withdrawn.

The foreman would take the hit, fined 20s and 20s costs. Farcical really as John and Philip stepped back into the workshop together before the end of that day's trading.

On the same day in court, a certain trader John Harvey 59, of Ann Street was summoned for exposing margarine for sale without a label attached! After hearing all the evidence, the Judge Mr Nagle said he did not see how a purchaser could be 'taken in' and as there had only been a technical breach of the law, he would be inflicting a small fine of 10s.

Keeping the Sabbath. That was a tough one, Saturdays for Jews, Sundays for Christians. Most citizens belonging to one or other faith did follow the rules. Employers as always carry more responsibility than most, as providers. It was and is a matter of survival, families and employees to look after. Commercial laws were stringent and there was certainly a different protocol in society back then. As it happens many traders took their chances, whilst others watched with catlike stealth.

1912 BELFAST NEWS LETTER

"What is a toothbrush?"

A chemist on York Street Belfast was summoned for failing to observe the weekly half holiday on the 6th November. Allegedly accused of selling a toothbrush at 4.30 pm.

BREACHES of THE SHOP ACT of 1912

Headline said that he did not think anyone could claim that a toothbrush was a surgical appliance. For the defendant the meaning of 'medicine' and 'appliance' was quoted from the Oxford Dictionary.

Nothing being more talked about than teeth being the road to good health; contending therefore that a toothbrush came within the meaning of 'medical appliances'.

The majority of magistrates disagreed. That same day.

A hairdresser from Victoria Street, it was alleged, sold a bottle of hair dye

Wednesday 18th November at 8.10 pm. His defence claimed it was a scalp treatment for dandruff, therefore a medical appliance.

The Bench concurred.

Defendants in a long list of traders which made court that day had their cases dismissed under the Probation of Offenders Act, each being ordered to pay Court Costs.

Philip Leopold and Son made that list, earning a fine of 2s 6d plus costs.

As this order form detailing his business opening hours shows, it was inevitable he would be caught trading illegally at some point. No doubt avoiding prosecution many times and so it would be 30 years of wily trading before they found themselves in court again, alongside fellow bespoke tailors.

1943 17TH MARCH BELFAST NEWSLETTER
"OLD STYLE SUITS"

Fifteen tailoring firms summoned and fined ten shillings and court costs of £2.2 shillings.

The crime, breeches of the Austerity Clothing Order which prohibited too many pockets in suits, and making trousers with turn-ups! Imagine!

How could he not have made that list?

Competition in the trade was fierce, still is, survival is the name of the game. The biggest difference? All manufacture and production was home based. The high levels of employment UK wide never before witnessed as the Industrial Revolution took hold.

Many individuals with vision established new styles of trading, saw avenues for new types of business and as the wider population started to earn money no matter how small their income was, entrepreneurs were born.

Philip would meet one of them. After initially arriving in Hull, England, and then travelling to Leeds for work, ensconced in the rag trade, his path would cross that of Michael Marks, a fellow Jew and immigrant well on his way to establishing himself in business. He was the influencer, a success story who made an impression on the not so simple message boy. The synagogue would prove a perfect meeting place not just for prayer. Although a life cut short very young, Michael Marks along with his partner Tom Spencer were market stall traders who laid foundations for a business which would through Marks' son become a global enterprise.

Socially, how could Philip not make friends? He was inoffensive, his religion was his to own, a life built around fashion. He reached out to people, and they embraced him, passionate about all things, believing without realising as they say the person who says it cannot be done, should not interrupt the person doing it.

Clothes do maketh the man, for some, they also provide a livelihood.

THE TERRORS IN FIELDS OF
SLAUGHTER AND DESOLATION

The Leopolds by this time had been living nearly 20 years in Belfast, working in an industrial boom and amongst all the Irish civil battles, which they quite possibly would not have fully understood, nor joined in. Now the current veil of unprincipled politics, heightened social unrest and conflict descended not just on home ground but across Europe. This atmosphere of terror engulfed everyone. Dark years.

The world was in the grip of WWI, and the island of Ireland was still part of the British Empire. Deeply divided religious faiths as in Catholics and Protestants would willingly fight side by side under the command of the British military, with the loss of tens of thousands of loyal soldiers fulfilling their duty to their country as unimaginable bloodshed was suffered in the fight of opposing Empires to claim supremacy. It was truly a pathetic slaughter. Historical documents report the grim days for those of poor means who were swept up by nationalist propaganda. Over 200,000 men from Ireland fought in the Great War. About 30,000 died serving in Irish regiments of the British forces and about 49,000 died altogether. This war unleashed a scale of violence never before witnessed in any previous conflict. Modern weaponry discharged an assault of cruel carnage. Losses on all fronts for the year 1914 topped five million, with a million men killed. The insurmountable level of casualties sustained in open warfare across land, called for death defying measures galvanising soldiers on all fronts to protect themselves. Their solution, dug outs, bunkers or as it was to become known,

THE FRONT-LINE TRENCHES

These mud-walls of physical protection laid way to a camaraderie rooted in loyalty, courage and determination mixed with desperate fear of death and uncertainty. Battle-weary soldiers came to believe they were 'all in it together'. Death or glory.

Irishmen of all persuasions, in the face of the enemy stood firmly with their fellow countrymen on a foreign battleground.

Then tragically on their return from the war zone, triumphant in the knowledge they had defeated the aggressors, they landed on home territory into a Civil War. Only to find themselves in a home grown 'no man's land'. Many shell-shocked, wounded and mentally broken. Equally celebrated yet relinquished in the new political arena, unable to escape their own profoundly moving struggle. A generation of broken souls.

The fight for Irish independence against the fight for British rule in 1916 was relaunched in earnest.

Hell descended on this island. Class division, loyalties and a shift in nationalism fed by a new breed of politicians provoked widespread resistance to a new proposed order of national conscription. The citizens of Ireland were torn apart by personal allegiance, faith and patriotism. The dark days of Irish history after the desolation of the famine, hit a new high. Could it get worse? It could. Simultaneously a tempered flu virus spread across Ireland at the beginning of 1918, only to return with a vengeance across the world that autumn, lasting until 1919. Military formations and homecoming troops were recognised as being the super spreaders of their day. All of Ireland would suffer from this epidemic as it raged indiscriminately, adding over 25,000 victims to that collective era of conflict, shockingly 50 million worldwide. A hundred years later strangely the end of 2019, marks the beginning of this century's Covid virus pandemic, globally recognised by governments this time as a war in itself, against all humanity.

By the end of the war 1918, in Ireland, Irish republicans won the general election and declared Irish Independence, triggering the Irish War of Independence 1919–22 through to the brutal Irish Civil War 1922–23 The final outcome seeing the partition of Ireland and the creation of the Irish Free State. The North held onto its status within the United Kingdom, a derisive situation for Nationalists, but a result Unionists welcomed. Tragically all over Ireland families by circumstance, some with no hard opinions just trying to live were forever displaced.

The Jewish Community lived both North and South of the border. Even the Leopolds found themselves caught up in the land division.

By the turn of the century Philip's nephew Alec, his brother Barrie's son, had left Kriukai and brought a little of Russia back to him in Belfast. In his willingness to belong he enlisted in the North Irish Regiment fighting for King and country in WW1 and following his uncle's lead would also change his name from Lepar to Leopold. As nature dictates it seems Alec set his sights on a Dubliner. Sofie Baker who more than impressed him. She too was a tailor and despite the opportunities Belfast offered, they chose to be closer to her parents eventually settling in Eire, not so far away as they saw it. At no time ever, would the Leopold family bond, face a challenge that this generation would allow to divide them. Not even as it would turn out, two world wars or a civil war on home ground and by the way Sofie was Jewish of course.

Nevertheless, by 1923 fragile peace descended, as N. Ireland moved into a new era. Ever present simmering social and political difficulties measured out on this beautiful land beyond the end of the twentieth century, yet, exceptionally at this juncture in time and remarkably in the midst of continuous conflict, Belfast was winning the stakes in industry, culture and future prospects.

Philip, Rose and their young brood were living and working through this new terror, right on their doorstep; at the heart of it, not their battle.

Embedded economically in the neighbourhood now. This time their religion was probably their best weapon of defence, coupled with a poor grasp of the English language. They, like many, simply wanted peace to give their families a good life.

Now fully Northern Irish Jews in spirit, enjoying good relations with their neighbours, simply weaving through the streets of Belfast, known as the foreigner tailors, holding their own good hand of cards, offering employment not only in their factory but through a web of outworkers.

Somehow they had managed to fit in.

Philip had loyalty to the land he had made his home for his wife and children. When he settled in Belfast, all of Ireland was part of the British Empire. He was a Northerner.

It was now 1925 time to claim new roots. Not remotely hesitant of what had happened to Otto Jaffa, he wanted official residency.

Conversations in broken English commenced, a direction was planned, as the saying goes, we are all only three phone calls away from the prime minister. The basis of success would be judged on character.

John Arnold, his former boss of some 15 years, guided all proceedings.

Two gentlemen collaborators of the tailoring kind, sparked by the first jaunt early in their work relationship, in front of a judge in the Law Courts. That was long forgotten, perhaps simply their version of the truth. For sure they came close to the legal line a good few times over the ensuing work years with roles eventually reversing in time. John, as retirement beckoned, knew Philip was ready to go it alone and handed the mantle to him. Between them, they saluted the establishment of the Philip Leopold workshop on Upper Donegal Street. He was Philip's secret weapon of defence.

The sponsors lined up. Another member of Arnold's staff, James Crowe, who had been assistant tailor to Philip when he had risen to manager in the company, added his support.

Then within easy reach, Thomas Neill, who deftly attended to a loyal clientele with his acute barbering skills, was open for business a few doors away from the Leopold shop on the Oldpark Road. The hair fraternity, commonly understood to be the greatest source of news and advice. Thomas or Mr Neill as Mr Leopold and he would have acknowledged each other, was honoured to be asked to stand as a referee. Their animated conversations would have evolved over Philip's many visits to his barber chair for a fresh cut throat razor shave and a standing appointment for his hair to be singed. A gentleman's luxury.

Finally James R Kelly, a dairy proprietor who lived in the same area as the family completed the inner circle. Those were the days when milk was delivered to your home and your milkman knew your name.

As documentation describes their character, in the language of the day, the importance of all these good and respectable men became of huge significance. They had lived on a land together as neighbours, all Irishmen, then through the partition of Ireland, and the Civil War and by 1921 geography dictated they were now officially British citizens. Except for Philip Leopold.

Well that was unacceptable to him, so with these friends standing as his referees following due process, he attained his British naturalisation.

By 1925 they were all legally British citizens, not English, Scottish or Welsh but proud Northern Irishmen and women, full of strong personalities, untethered opinions, drama and competition. A family of eight children under the keen eye and control of their parents. There was a lot to talk about, they were socialisers, seven spoiled princesses and a prince who would follow a strict routine.

'School', 'Dada's Workshop' and 'Home' at least for these early years. Then these young damsels grew up and this story gathers edge, bigger parts for some more than others, although all will make an appearance.

KISMET

Belfast 1930: Lightning struck and the earth rocked as destiny stepped in across the religious divide, this time it was between Catholic and Jew.

Tommy Rolston, a youth from Fermanagh, looking for work found himself in Belfast, with 'A' political views, only familiar with the congenial fellow countrymen of his hometown Lisnarick, Irvinestown. Tommy seized his opportunity and joined the RUC.

He was now in the Big Smoke. A handsome devil unleashed onto the streets of the City.

Stationed at Glenravel Police Station, North Queen Street, Tommy embraced his new life as a constable.

Neska Leopold, the sixth daughter of Philip and Rose Leopold and Tommy Rolston were to become an item.

Little did he know he had been spotted by a terrorist in a silk dress.

As it happened one of his duties would place him on Points Duty on Lower Donegall Street, a well-trodden path.

One day as she left her father's workshop Neska Leopold caught sight of Tommy Rolston.

As he ushered her safely across the road, her heart stopped as they exchanged glances.

Tommy was never getting away from her, she set her heart on him! He just had to fall in love with her. Religion, what religion?

Neska refused to give him up, no one was listening, never imagining her capacity for defiance. No you can't have. Says who?

She, like her siblings, was spoiled and even worse she was in love.

This young damsel only heard her own voice and made her own rules. What she would or would not do with indifference.

"Neska, your turn to wash the back stairs."

Oh yeah, as she defiantly stood at the top, out of sight and flung a basin of water down them.

"What's all the squealing about?"

As the neighbours' unsuspecting cat ran for cover having been swung round by its tail and hurled over the back garden wall by the bold young Leopold. However it had offended her.

Punishment; lie over dada's knee, have your tokus slapped and then kiss dada's hand. Not bite it!

This adolescence was her makeup, forever and a day.

Secretly, an incredulous plan was hatched between Neska and Tommy.

They made preparations with Tommy's parish priest, Father Joseph Bryne, set a date, and quietly kept this ceremony only to themselves. Besotted with each other and as desperately as she would have wanted everyone to celebrate with them, the couple would not change their minds.

1st December 1930, as the city bustled with life, time almost stood still for Neska Leopold. Standing alone in the doorway of the chapel, she hesitated slightly, heart racing with mixed emotions. It had to be this way and so it was to pass, this diminutive rebel in high heels stepped down the aisle to meet the man of her dreams.

Tommy Rolston elegantly turned his broad shoulders as he gazed down at her and smiled reassuringly into her dancing eyes. They exchanged marital vows at the altar of the side chapel Saint Joseph's in St. Patrick's Chapel inconceivably which stood next door to her father's workshop. Had they harboured wishes that maybe someone from the family would happen upon them? Stand with them and celebrate their day. Sadly that was not to be. They would share it with the closest of their close friends. Tommy's best man, a fellow officer, none other than Philip Coulter whose musical genius of a son was not even a twinkle in his eye at that time and along with him Sarah Magee, a cousin of Tommy's from Fermanagh. Tommy was 27, Neska was 21 and a half, so the marriage certificate reads.

Three days later nothing else for it they made the announcement.

The walls virtually caved in at the Leopolds. Had she lost her mind?

So many opinions are not in her favour I am afraid. No celebrations.

Although to some it meant death as the chief Rabbi came calling to add to the grief. He in his honesty and faith believed the way forward for the family was for her father to say the Dead Prayers over her.

The parents were challenged and they needed to restore harmony, this would be too much for Philip and Rose. Dada would decide the outcome.

Harmony did return, they, as always forgave.

Philips' faith remained his family's sense of identity, yet there was a line he would not cross. He could bear it.

"I cut off my right arm before I would lose my daughter, in fact you can take all of me"; a quote referred to many times within the home.

She for her part might have married out of the faith, she too had the shoulders to bear that and the spirit.

The sisters and brother would see it differently. Such defiance was nearly unheard of in 1930, especially from a daughter even if they had been raised to be independent.

They loved her and were mad at her in the same breath, why?

How could they really argue, sure they all knew and loved Tommy Rolston, especially Philip and Rose. He had never been a secret and was already part of their lives, with no hidden agenda and of course they could see it was a love match.

It was not just Neska who claimed him as "My Tommy, My Tommy."

Tommy now belonged to them.

Secretly, 60 years later, guarded whispers admitted there were private gatherings amongst her siblings for such prayers to be said. Neska would never know that or maybe she was told and kept it to herself.

Within the year the newlyweds welcomed their daughter Beryl into the world, born on the day after their first anniversary.

Dada was present at her birth, more than anxious for his daughter, he booked her into a private nursing home on Limestone Road, Belfast. Well aware of the trauma his Rose had endured in her childbearing years when luxuries were few and far between.

So now meet the heart of this novella. A child who was only eight years of age when WWII broke out, an innocent whose life began in extraordinary circumstances and whose formative years witnessed war, curfew and a family upbringing like none of her peers.

The link between the past and the present. Living many lives.

Was she Jewish, was she Protestant, was she Catholic?

For a long time in the dark. In fact I could nearly be sure she coined the phrase

"Daddy, is the pope a Catholic?"

The very serious question of the Irish in Ireland, she innocently asked of him one day after school. Not about the pope, about your religion.

His reply, "I wouldn't know, my love."

Wondering to himself where she had heard such a thing.

The Jewish relatives humorously kept the quandary going.

"Who knows? Nobody seems to know!"

As she grew up, it became apparent other inherent attributes from her father and grandfather were common sense and a healthy memory.

Those vivid recollections of the adults in her life fashioned her, making their mark.

There were no dull characters, just more time spent with some.

BERYL

Behind those eyes a sweet soul breathes
Honest in every way
"Thank God for my life and all that I have"
She would forever humbly would say

– Geraldine Connon

NESKA'S SISTERS BEA AND DOROTHY
THE FREEMAN HOUSEHOLD

Beryl's memories of her eldest aunts

Bea, born 1901, was the first child of the Leopolds. Tall and elegant, taking her role as the eldest very seriously as she grew up, content in knowing her sisters respected her say-so.

Right from the get-go, nearly as soon as she could walk, Dada had her hanging onto his coat tails. The tailoring profession was at its height, a huge network of people throughout the UK especially within the Jewish immigrants from Eastern Europe. It was not only employment, it was a social scene and it was the greatest avenue to enable that most favourite challenge of Jewish parents, to match their children off well.

Of course when that time would arrive.

Bea was to make an appearance from a very young age at her father's work, he loved to show her and her sisters off. John Arnold the boss and his wife looked with great favour on her father enjoying his attitude to life. They would always protect him and his family.

THE EMPLOYEES of the CORNHILL NORTH STREET BELFAST SOCIAL

The Weekly Telegraph, Saturday, January 27 1912,

THE MODEL CAFE DONEGAL STREET BELFAST

The evening went something like this as the editorial reads. Saluting the camaraderie of the workforce of Arnold's tailors, whilst displaying the social respect and manners towards kith and kin prevalent of the day.

Once the host had extended a cordial welcome to his guests Mr James Crowe [manager] thanked Mr Arnold for his generous hospitality and toasted the success of the 'House' during the past year. He then opened the floor to others present who also spoke in eulogistic terms of Mr Arnold and his wife. These speakers were Mr John Dolan [under manager], Mr A.Gilmore [principal cutter] and Mr P. Leopold.

For sure this would have brought smiles and humour to the guests as

Philip, compelled to thank his boss, would not have allowed his broken English to hold him back, drawing applause and cheers all around.

The programme for the evening had such a headliner.

The Leopolds would not have been able to sit still.

Opening performance; Miss B. Leopold, song.

Miss M. Instance, recitation; Miss BB. Buchanan, song and recitation; Miss E Lavine, song; Mr John M'Avoy, song and ragtime dances;

Mr H. Nixon, song; Mr H. Fulton, biographical sketches;

Messrs Henry & Austin, comedians; Mr E. Purvis & "Battling Tom" songs.

Followed by games most likely parlour board games from table to table.

Mrs Arnold provided and presented prizes to the winners.

This gives an essence of working and social life amongst those of the rag trade and strikingly it shows the importance of family as Bea Leopold, Philip's 11-year-old daughter was to sing as part of the evening's entertainment. It also shows the respect which was growing amongst John and Philip, as his young Jewish assistant pattern cutter alongside.

The journalism of the day concluded the report as: Before terminating the proceedings, Mr Gilmore proposed a comprehensive vote of thanks, seconded by Mr John Mc Laughlin and passed by hearty acclamation.

Mr Sam McGarrell rendered valuable services on the piano.

Bea would have made Dada proud this night, she would have been wearing a new dress, only to be expected.

The Leopold girls would enjoy being fussed over by the ladies on the factory floor, they would have had, as they say, friends in high places. Wardrobes of handmade clothes which caused a flurry of attention every time they made an appearance. Especially as they grew in numbers.

It was only within a few fleeting years from childhood to becoming a young lady that a dashing tailor would introduce himself to her.

No doubt he had already asked her father if that would be appropriate and of course permission was granted.

On the 20th August 1919, Bea would happily marry Samuel Freeman, the second son of Mr J Freeman who hailed from Leeds. Sam, an accomplished tailor by trade, would join forces with his father-in-law.

It was not even a year after the Great War.

Her parents were very happy with this match, holding Sam with the highest regard, he fitted well with the family. This was the first of the Leopold girls' weddings and a precedent was set.

The ceremony took place in the synagogue, on Annesley Street by the Rev. Dr D. I. Herzog. M.A. assisted by the Rev. Barnett and the Rev. Myerovit along with a joyous gathering of the community which had grown in numbers since the turn of the century. By December Herzog, the Chief Rabbi of Belfast, was appointed to serve in Dublin.

North Belfast neighbourhood relations were so good when it came to the case of weddings, all Jewish receptions at that time were held in the local Orange Hall on Clifton Street, Belfast. That was something.

So, the newlyweds began married life moving into their first home on Alliance Avenue near home. Then as business improved Sam and she moved to Cliftonville Road. Great excitement ensued as they awaited the birth of their first born unaware of the challenge they would face. Unexpectedly, their first-born child Dorothy who, cosseted with constant care, was fragile and handicapped. It was a worry then, as is now for parents, all consuming, yet most likely somewhat more fearful for a first-time mother in a time of so little public health assistance.

Then within a year, the young couple welcomed their son Leslie into their lives, the worshipped first son and grandson of the new generation.

Once again such happiness rained down. Bea cared for them all in the home, while the workshop claimed Sam's daily routine. When he returned home every evening, sometimes late into the twilight hours, he always looked in on his children as they slept. Bea would then quietly get the chance to sit for a while and gather her own thoughts whilst listening to Sam softly sing a lullaby for Dorothy should she be awake or asleep. This was a ritual they shared throughout her life. It is now 1928. The Freemans were complete.

DOLLY LEOPOLD

The sister who broke hearts.

Well hello Dolly born 1902, second in line to the kingdom.

Undeniably delightful Dolly.

As it happens stunning looks as a child transformed into the shape of an alluring young woman. Living up to her polished appearance and gift of effortless style, which had not gone unnoticed by the family, Dada could see a future for her in fashion. He of course would help financially and with his connections in the trade.

So it came to be, Dolly was to follow her passion and became the proprietress of a ladies fashion shop on York Street, surrounded by beaus and hopeful suitors who routinely fell under the spell of her fair magic. It was now the Roaring Twenties.

Often in passing, a shy soft-spoken gentleman would tip his hat at her as he walked to work in a local dairy, none other than James R Kelly's. That gentleman happened to be Tommy Rolston's uncle who could never muster his nerve to introduce himself to her, even though he assuredly told his young nephew that she was his girlfriend. A Rolston was surely destined to meet and marry a Leopold. It was not to be him.

Dolly was courted by Harry Cohen, finally accepting his proposal of marriage.

Nothing could have been more exciting for her, she had full rein to plan and organise this affair along with the finesse.

It was the talk of the Community, the style was crushing, somewhat like a fairytale. Dolly and Harry settled down to married life, looking forward to their future.

Then, as the twenties drew to an end, the thirties brought them children, two daughters named Gladys and Jacqueline. All was good, not a whisper of the kiss of death.

SAMUEL (SONNY) LEOPOLD

Enough about the girls, what about the boy?

Sonny appeared in 1915. The level of excitement could not be measured. A son, at last, a son.

He was the seventh child and was worshipped immediately by his parents. Born with a silver spoon in his mouth. Not only did he have the attention of his parents, once his sisters forgave him for being born he inherited six other advisors. Maybe this was the reason when he found his own voice that he became so outspoken. Subtlety was definitely not one of his strengths. He was outrageous. As it happened more and even more so with age, he would never mellow. Well known for untethered opinions and dismissal of his adversaries. A favourite quip of his being, "Watch him! He can hear round corners," or if he was asked not to say something he would grandly announce "I'll be diplomatic" as if he was doing a favour. One of his most staggering turns in his seniority, when he resided in a private nursing home, followed an event in the synagogue. Sonny sent word to one of the ladies of the community, proclaiming he needed to talk to her urgently. So dutifully this softly spoken lady arrived to visit him, concerned as to what was so pressing. Sonny simply said that he was sorry to have to tell her this but he had noticed and had she not realised herself, that she had gained a lot of weight! He had a unique ability to leave people standing aghast with his remarks, to him it was frankly a matter of fact. 'The Times they were a changing', as the lady left never to return.

So in his heyday dressed off the best, well-heeled and with his father's blessing he had the where for all, along with his friends to frequent the Jewish Club and maybe further afield. Opinionated, outspoken male chauvinists, dangerous in numbers.

Lock up your daughters.

Destined to join his father's business, he accepted that the rag trade was where his future lay, yet in his later life he recognised that he would have made a better lawyer. Not even fit to sew a button on, his gift was he could talk shop and with the strength of the tailors' workshop behind him, life was sweet for Sonny. He was free to strike deals and emboldened as production always delivered on promises. Sonny, like his siblings, enjoyed the fruits of their parents' success and in their youth afforded them boundless freedom socially and financially.

1925–39 BELFAST, UPPER DONEGAL STREET

The Leopold workshop was in full flight and by 1925 employed 47 staff. Only those who work in the rag trade would remotely comprehend that commitment, the skill, the endless work hours. The highs and lows. The grief and the glory. Philip loved the business. He loved his workers, they loved him, simply calling him Boss. Hence, they all richly earned the title of high-class tailors, living to the soundtrack of sewing machines, overlockers and steam presses.

Philip and his accountant Miss Smith had a special friendship. She was in fact not a Miss, mistakenly thinking he would not employ a married woman. As he would have said "Not mein business".

Every week they played out a game when it came to balancing the company takings and every week it had the same outcome.

Miss Smith would put her hand over the final tally and the Boss would confirm it without fail. He would have calculated it in his head.

Luck followed them for more than 40 years. Seems it is true, you cannot have everything all the time. As life as we know it goes, all good things come to an end. Inexplicably with the curse of joy comes the sharpness of sorrow, it's unexpected strike always cruel. Back in 1931 when the family swore that Neska's marriage out of 'the faith' was unforgivable, they came to witness that storyline pale into insignificance. It was all on the turn now, despite another successful Jewish match.

TAILOR'S TAILORS

The greatest social network of the day. Better still it was face to face. What a clear and present shot for marriage proposals. It was for most of the Leopolds anyhow. Closest in years and firm friends of Neska was darling Auntie Mille, so humorous and dry witted yet quite the opposite in nature. Much more serious in her ways and in her youth very sensible.

Who did she happen to find herself in love with? None other than an Englishman who hailed from Leeds, where his father owned, would you believe it another tailor's atelier. Albert Coss appeared on the scene looking for a bride. Seems despite our land's endless turbulence the Jewish fraternity loved to travel to these shores. In Albert's case he could live with it, for shockingly in his youth he had seen much worse.

Born in 1900 into a close immigrant Jewish family, he from any age was an adventurer. He did not need any encouragement to take a dare, so by the time he reached his teens, working as a message boy was not really cutting it for him. Then on his rounds running errands the impressionable young boy stopped in his tracks. Staring down from the city walls nearly on every street corner were War propaganda posters screaming at him,

Albert was transfixed by the most famous recruitment poster of them all, the iconic portrait of the British Secretary of State for War and the words:

LORD KITCHENER WANTS ME

Innocently, albeit naively in his own words, he in later life recollected, "Give it a go Joe, I didn't give a damn about anything. I was a fool, I wanted excitement, I wanted something to do."

1915 Albert was destined for the frontline trenches in Arras Germany, stationed there throughout an extreme winter only to be sent home to England and discharged when his parents informed the army of his real age, 15. Disregarding this horrific experience of Germany's first use of chlorine gas, Albert re-enlisted this time to the Royal Artillery. Lying once again about his age and probably his name this time. Ending up on the Front in Belgium and France. Fighting there until the end of the war and remaining in the Army until 1922. A survivor.

When he left the army just like thousands of young men he was changed forever. Of course he had lost his youth, fatefully not his life.

Albert came home to a grateful caring mother and father. Their quest to bring normality back into his life, for them all to have peace and find a future for their son.

"Find a nice girl, settle down, have a family. Don't you see this for you?" the parents cried.

Well of course he did. Even though it took him over ten years to get the army experience out of his system. He would recognise his second chance for a different life.

Now where was his future wife?

Well sure wasn't she in Belfast, one of Philip Leopold's younger daughters.

Following his future father-in-law's steps with numerous trips across the pond, the courting began. Albert, as it happens, was already known to the family. Their paths had crossed numerous times, maybe more so in social circles, so he was not a stranger. You could hardly write it, lo and behold another match was made.

Albert asked Philip for his daughter's hand in marriage and on approval proposed to Millie.

She accepted with such unreserved glee. It was now her turn as their wedding hit the talk of the synagogue and this time there was a dainty bridesmaid on hand. Dolly's youngest daughter Jacqueline, quietly smiling yet secretly enjoying her place in the official portraits as any child would.

That would be the chat for months afterwards. It is now the mid 30s.

Oh how brutal change was coming to everyone

The entire narrative of the Leopolds changed forever.

Completely unexpectedly, and yet she had such strength, on the 4th October 1935 Rose suddenly became unwell, the faithful wife and mother always in the background, who too had carried such responsibility, died of heart failure in her husband's arms. Aged 59.

"For God's sake look how happy and well she looked in her recent photograph with dad. Why should this be?" Everyone cried.

The suddenness is unbearable.

This match of Russian birth, made in Belfast, lived in honesty and hard work, intense in love and sacrifice was struck out.

Philip was distraught. His faith taught him that there was life after death, he would have to strive hard to hope for it.

ROSE

Do not look into my eyes I am in pain
I have lost my spirit I am nearly insane
For the moment I'm fragile, I have little to say
Be gentle with my heart dear God I pray

– Geraldine Connon

Within nine days of the death, Millie would give birth to a daughter.

Millie who was in the last stages of her pregnancy and confined to her bed, bewildered as to why her mother was not coming to visit.

Amongst the tears of joy mixed tears of grief as she and Albert became the proud parents to Rose named for her grandmother.

A child who would never meet her namesake.

THE COSS HOUSEHOLD

Nerves are shattered as no one could find peace from the distress of losing Rose. A new level of normality played out. The Coss's bid for independence now changed. Dada needed to be cared for and they took up residence in the family home with Millie taking on the role as official housekeeper. Their new baby brought joy and hope for brighter days.

The house became even more of a draw to all the siblings as they clung to memories of their mother and nervously supported their broken father.

It took time but humour and fight would return to them, driven by their own children as they grew up under tight scrutiny.

"Ladies don't cross their legs. Ladies don't put their elbows on the table. Ladies don't whistle." and so it went on, sounding out to childish ears.

"I don't think I want to be a lady," Beryl would have exclaimed.

Millie and Neska would witness their daughters become the closest of all the cousins. Two very different girls, Rose confidently being more daring than Beryl and when they became teenagers slightly more likely to defy the rules. The girls were full of romance and of course Roses' biggest infatuation was the entertainer Frankie Vaughan.

When he performed at the Opera House in Belfast there sat the two of them in the audience, Rose in raptures staring adoringly, willing him to invite her up onto the stage and serenade her.

Damn it some other lucky girl caught his attention.

Why had they not been sitting in those seats?

Of course, drama was never far away, it was inherited.

On a shopping trip into town it had to be cut short and the girls were marched home.

Rose had used the F-word! Taught by her friend Charlie Watson who lived on Kingsmere Ave.

Millie and Bea were aghast, lamenting on the company she had been keeping whilst reaching Neska, a cool glass of water at the kitchen table to help her recover from the shock, as she felt quite faint.

Rose was sent to bed. It was never deliberate; she was simply innocent and impressionable. Everything for her was in honesty, like the time Dada hosted dinner for an extremely elegant family from Dublin to entertain a possible match for Sonny and when her mother asked her what on earth was she doing as she rubbed her back against the dining room door frame because it was itchy. She replied, "Sure that's what you do mum."

That match never stood a chance.

All these antics of course only made the girls closer, they made pacts with each other. When the aunts tried their hand at matchmaking Rose would create a fuss so she could go to the cinema too and would just have to sit in between her cousin and the latest suitor.

What next?

Even though all the adults smoked, which was the done thing in those days, when Beryl decided to give it a go in Rose's bedroom, choking herself trying to be modern, their hearts stopped when they heard Millie racing up the stairs.

"Are you two smoking in there?" was the accusing rhetoric echoing up the landing.

"No, no," the girls shouted, eyes wide, deftly placing the cigarette on the window sill.

Millie brushed into the room as was her right, taking in the visions in front of her pretending to be painting their nails. Menacingly she walked over to the window. Spinning round she asked, "Are you going to spend all day up here? Why don't you take yourselves out and get some fresh air," and then she breezed out of the room.

A few minutes later when the dust settled the girls edged over to the window bewildered as to where the cigarette was. Hells bells, it had rolled off the ledge. Looking down into the courtyard there was Granda looking up at them with a knowing smile. He had heard the commotion unfolding and happened to be in the garden. He just lifted up his foot and there it was.

The truth of it all, the girls were their mothers reincarnated.

Back in the day when Philip's sister Alma came to visit from Kriukai, Neska was charged with escorting her shopping around the local delicatessen shops. When the proprietor of the fruit shop met her parents later in the week she recounted with some humour that Neska had taught this very beautiful woman to ask for,

"A dozen of oranges you bliddy bitch."

Neska was never the ringleader amongst her sisters but she did chase a dare. All the girls frequented the workshop after school most days, possibly with the parents' wish that one of them might catch the tailoring bug, sadly that would not be the case. They did love the buzz, it was a hive of activity. Of course there were opportunities for other devilment.

Sometimes the temptation was too much. Swept up by the latest in vogue dance, what better stage could be right in front of her. Flirting with the rather attractive tailor's apprentice, Neska and he were caught dancing the Charleston up and down the cutting table in between patterns and cloth when Dada appeared in the doorway. They were so wrapped up in the dance they did not even notice him for a few seconds. As her sisters looked on laughing and encouraging her, after all no point in dancing unless you have an audience, it all instantly came to a halt. Eyes flashing between them in silence. "Off the table! Now!" was the command. Neska got a clip round the legs and was sent home to bed.

Her accomplice sacked. There was plenty of hushed chat and giggling amongst the girls that night. The apprentice showed up the next morning with his mother to ask for his job back which of course he got.

In Beryl's words, he was reinstated.

1939 OUTBREAK OF WORLD WAR TWO

So a new era began in the Leopold household, Rose was at peace, the family were learning to live without her. United in grief, they would need strength because this level of pain would hit them again and again.

There was a measure of mercy giving them a few years to recover as it played out, yet life as they knew it was ending, cruelly.

On September 1st 1939 Hitler invaded Poland from the West, two days later France and Britain declared war on Germany and WWII began.

On September 17 Soviet troops invaded Poland from the East.

Once again the world sank into an abyss. This time, the sinister dictatorship of Hitler regressed into never as seen before crimes against humanity on many levels.

The Jewish Community in Belfast closed ranks. Shrouded in fear once again. Was their safe haven at risk, would their adopted neighbours desert them? Definitely not. Irish people of all creeds would unite, despite in effect the South declaring neutrality. There was a vicious common enemy, wholly dangerous and determined in their pursuit of world dominance. A path for a common ground of defence had to be agreed. That would take politicians and deal makers many months initially as party politics and government found themselves scrambling in response to a battleground which Hitler and his army chiefs had been laying plans for since the outcome of WWI. A hellish time amongst the Allies trying to pre-empt enemy military manoeuvres whilst exercising a national campaign on the Home Front in response.

The following paragraphs set the scene as it played out historically, an initial nightmare for political decisions, orders and disagreements.

The Leopolds in Belfast and Dublin and the Rolstons in Fermanagh and Larne along with their neighbours waited and listened for direction.

Viscount Craigavon Prime Minister of Northern Ireland and Head of the Unionist party declared in the House of Commons on the 4th September 1939 that Northern Ireland was in a state of war and along with the entire

United Kingdom would face all the responsibilities imposed on its citizens.

World Service, radio, cinemas all laid bare the perilous state of affairs for everyone to witness and understand. The N. Irish looked to their government for leadership and direction.

For some, the war was the only talk of conversation. None more so than those in the Jewish Community who through their own network of communication could foresee an escalation of the antisemitism Hitler and his Nazi Party had sinisterly commenced as early as 1933.

The Leopolds had by now been in Belfast over 40 years.

The older generation still might not have spoken fluent English, their children did, yet collectively the wider community fully understood it.

No one raised the subjects more than Sonny, always in the center of the debate of politics, welfare, employment, business, the lot, in their homes, the Jewish Club, the synagogue, with their friends and their neighbours. If Hitler won, they were all doomed.

As always in this Province, although part of the United Kingdom and having our own government, opposing religions and politics both internal and external continued to set out old boundaries, grievances and disagreements.

Hence from 1939 through even until 1941, N. Ireland was sinking in unemployment and still suffering from the economic and industrial downturn following WWI and despite political and business efforts in general it seemed to many here that we were not at war. Even well-placed politicians in London lamented that the sirens in N. Ireland had hardly been sounded five times since the outbreak of the war.

Emphatically a major part of the problem for N. Ireland was the way in which powers were divided between Belfast and London under the Government of Ireland Act of 1920 and the Anglo-Irish Treaty of 1921.

A political quagmire. Just a little bit of research reveals that surprisingly by the end of 1940 Northern Ireland was not represented on the Production Council, the Labour Supply Board, the Economic Policy Committee or the Industrial Capacity Committee.

Nor had the Province secured the building of one or other Royal Ordnance Factories.

The repercussions of this were twofold.

The Northern Ireland government was depleted in its ability to lobby effectively on behalf of businesses leaving industry and manufacture here with very little voice and the internal commercial battle to win lucrative government contracts on the outbreak of war was fought hard by those closest to London. Even by 1941 those N. Irish most desperate for employment would have to migrate to Britain for work.

Stormont continued with bitter debate and criticism from backbenchers.

In 1920 the IRA had launched a bombing campaign in Britain, then just before the outbreak of this war they suddenly launched into a fresh anti-government bombing campaign in 1940 both in N. Ireland and Britain, feeding anti-Irish sentiment on the mainland, coupled with civil unrest and fears at home. In this heightened tension, particularly concentrated in Derry and Belfast, the Unionist government under the directive of the Minister of Home Affairs, Dawson Bates who had already introduced internment on 22nd Dec 1938, exercised these powers now on a much wider scale. This grim internal chaos and all-round dissent could possibly have also contributed to the failure of the N. Ireland government efforts in securing economic investment.

Incandescent in the background of the political arena in Belfast and totally committed to the allied victory was staunch Ulster Unionist Viscount Basil Brookeborough, a survivor of the British Empire military campaign in WWI, avid anti-Home Ruler and organiser of the Fermanagh Vigilance. By 1929 he returned to Parliament and four years later joined the cabinet as Minister of Agriculture, a position he held up to and during the initial stages of the war. Significantly by 1941 he became Minister of Commerce and finally in this caustic atmosphere N. Ireland moved into organised war production under his leadership.

Critically, as those on the ground witnessed in his previous role of Minister of Agriculture, on a recruiting campaign to Derry City in August 1940, he assessed the atmosphere.

On the outbreak of war the directive from London declared there was to be no introduction of conscription in the Province, viewing that decision as the lesser of two evils following the rise in nationalist objections and fears of political and social unrest.

No one wanted Derry to go up in flames.

In October 1939, possibly from the shadows of the carnage of lives lost in WWI and as historical documents report, only a measured 2500 Northern Irish had joined the Armed Forces. Then allegiance to fellow countrymen awoke and as enemy warfare raged and advanced, these numbers would swell to 38,000 during the ensuing years of the conflict. This was in fact a remarkable effort considering that everyone was a volunteer and despite Eire remaining neutral from the outset, 43,000 Southern Irish people joined the British army.

In addition to that collective sacrifice on the battlefield, ultimately, N, Ireland would play a highly significant key role in all walks of life when military strategy advanced and the powers that be came to understand the value of the Province as a result of its geographical location. That reality only set in by 1941 when the Luftwaffe began their onslaught on these shores nearly two years into the war against a backdrop of civilian life where most by the bye did not believe they were engaged in a life nor death struggle.

THE WAR ARRIVES ON THE SHORES
OF NORTHERN IRELAND

The Belfast Blitz, apart from those in London, was the greatest loss of life in any night raid during the war.

Northern Ireland was ill prepared for such levels of bomb damage in the city as it highlighted all that was weak. Poor air defences and civil defence planning, the vulnerability of workers in their homes, civilians, power supplies, actual industrial capacity and even the running of the government. Mayhem ensued, mixed with grief, fear and loss.

The citizens of Belfast and outer suburbs fled from the city in their droves. Leaving about 20,000 sleeping out at night and thousands homeless.

A majority of solely working class from red brick houses, people with no luxuries and with even less now. Living in absolute disaster desperately in need of government direction and organised recovery assistance.

There were no names on the bombs as they fell indiscriminately on all. Catholics, Protestants or Jews, civilians or military. Now in the face of death and tragedy all survivors would join hands in serving in the civil defence services. Laying bare the indifference and parity of poverty to both politicians and citizens.

Social camaraderie would survive on this island for that time.

Northerners would flee en masse across the border for refuge.

In return Southern Ireland, although deemed as neutral in the conflict, for its part demonstrated immense sympathy and assistance for Belfast providing much needed support for Northern evacuees.

Effectively this was viewed by the Germans with observations by Dr Eduard Hempel, their minister in Dublin as the final breach of Ireland's neutrality. As an act of their frustration and retaliation the Luftwaffe in anger would then launch a bombing raid on the city of Dublin by the end of May 1941.

Civilian relations in all of Ireland for the interim gave hope that perhaps the North and South might find some common ground. Sadly no political leader could galvanize passions and make that peace.

How different lives on these lands would and could have been.

The Leopolds as did their neighbours in the city held their breath.

Destruction now raining down from the skies above them. What now? No defences, no protection, nowhere to hide and nowhere to run.

A voice screaming in his head tortured Philip as his mind turned to his missing daughter Neska who no longer lived nearby. With no means of contact as the skyline burnt red and thundered with the roll of plane engines and bombs, he and the rest of the family hunkered down in their home in Kingsmere Avenue.

Waiting in silence for it soon to be over, believing as they prayed it was in God's hands if they would escape death.

1941 LARNE ... THE ROLSTON HOUSEHOLD

Neska, Tommy and Beryl Rolston moved to the port of Larne from Belfast around 1938, looking for work and to set up home.

They settled on the Bank Road, just on the outskirts of the town and Tommy joined the bus service.

Even though within the year war was declared, life in the port did not dramatically change for the locals, just as life in the rest of the Province played out. War had not reached our shores with everything relatively normal. It would not remain that way.

The background to the next part of my story is taken from war reports "Attention girls".

When the war broke out significantly the return of the Treaty Ports to Eire in 1938 and the fall of France in 1940 meant it was safer for US ships to sail northwards via the sea route known as the Western Approaches past Northern Ireland to get to Britain than use the Southern route where German U-boats were efficiently sinking essential merchant supply ships to Britain from America. Without these imports, Britain was doomed.

Selected well-placed ports throughout the North proved highly successful and vital in averting disaster.

Just as that would happen.

Larne and Belfast by matter of location proved hugely significant in the War naval strategy becoming bases from which minesweepers and anti-submarine patrols protected the Irish Sea and the North Channel.

The Olderfleet Hotel at Larne Harbour consequently became the Naval Headquarters.

In June 1942 a Royal tour saw the King and Queen within their itinerary, visit Larne and be seen to support and raise morale of the military.

LIFE magazine would cover the story, printing a whole host of photographs of the Royal visit, following their traditional inspection of Royal Navy and United States Marines personnel on the roadside standing on ceremony at the front of the Hotel. A salubrious event for the North but even more so for the local residents.

Only a year earlier it had been quite a different storyline.

As Beryl and her friends walked to school the day after war was declared, their innocence spoke volumes. When discussing how long the war would last, Beryl suggested probably a fortnight. Her oldest friend in the group dismissed that saying it would be at least three years.

There was great excitement and a feeling of importance when a few months later the girls walked home with their newly issued gas masks slung over their shoulders. Naturally the novelty of them wore off pretty soon when in class the nuns would rehearse the drill daily.

It was a mixture of the unnerving shrill of the warning siren and the uncomfortable suffocating nature of the masks that took the shine of it.

So although Larne, a harbour and well situated was low key, crucially it also lay in a hollow and residents fastidiously followed strict blackout rules which saved it from all possible air attacks. It also lay directly in the flight path to Belfast meaning in 1941 when the German Luftwaffe began their onslaught in N. Ireland the sinister, doomful drone of German planes could be heard overhead as they progressed towards the city. These country people huddled down.

After the first attack, ARP (air raid protection) stepped up in the town. For those living in more exposed areas Tommy joined volunteer drivers to take those vulnerable people by bus into the countryside for safety. That left Beryl and her mum in their house which sat under the shelter of the Inver hills. As night drew in the following evening, nerves on edge, following an agreed plan with Tommy before he left on duty, his two ladies went to bed. They may have slept a little, anxiously waiting for the drone and then sure enough, there it came.

Hearts pounding, frozen with fear they took shelter under the stairs.

When silence descended in the early hours of the morning, mother and daughter ventured back upstairs to take a look.

The sky across the lough was lit up, blazing red. Belfast was burning. Neska was hysterical.

Was Tommy coming home? Was he injured? Was he dead? What about her parents, had they died?

The two of them waited in the house out of their wits with fear and then Tommy appeared through the door. If he was anxious he hid it well and within minutes they were back on the Bank Road.

Blinded with fear Neska could not hide her agitation from her daughter who quietly held her father's hand very tightly.

Public transport at a standstill, opportunity approached and in the eerie light of dawn Tommy flagged a lorry down agreeing with the driver to take Neska to Belfast.

Radio broadcasts were limited with any true information.

Finally when the driver turned onto Upper Donegal Street, her heart jumped. Screaming out to the driver to stop through her tear-stained face there he was.

"Dada! Dada!" she ran from the lorry into her father's arms.

He and Albert, his son-in-law, stopped in their stride, arms outstretched and caught her. They had been hurriedly making their way down towards the Shore Road to try and find transport, equally frightened, believing that in fact it was Larne that had been flattened in the raid. Neska had always been Dada's baby. Everyone was safe. Their house may have shook during the raid, the bedrooms taking the force of the blasts as ceilings cracked and plaster scattered over floors, on the upper landing and stairs, while the antique fireplaces fell out from the walls.

It would be chillingly, a temporary distraction from the impending doom that was looming.

1941 LEOPOLD AND SON WORKSHOP
IN THE WAR EFFORT

The impact of war had finally reached our shores. Uncertainty tainted everything.

The demographic of N. Ireland's citizens and workforce was under risk.

The course of business and survival of the fittest at the mercy of war became even more frenetic. It could be said, we were in a blue funk.

Business in these six counties apart from the large Belfast employers, hinged on cottage industries and manufacture, exactly the type that mostly lost out in rearmament and war contracts.

The hard facts reveal the Ministry of Supply in Britain 'simply could not be bothered' to deal with their need for immediate remuneration, preferring to deal with larger, solid firms, in particular factories in Britain familiar to London. To a degree this is understandable, it was a war situation which was evolving and changing on a daily basis justifying, apart from the priority of military decisions which were of tantamount importance, the government's preference to deal with big business players for their experience, as companies jostled to win these lucrative war contracts. With this deliberation it shows how in the run up to and the early years of the war, small companies in N. Ireland were at a grave disadvantage.

In 1940 there were only five firms on direct government contracts.

Philip Leopold amongst his business colleagues would have strongly debated this perilous scenario behind closed doors, his son Sonny was not prepared to sit quietly. He had found his voice as a child, when he needed to speak with confidence to be heard over his seven animated sisters. A talent he perfected with his extreme politeness. His career should have been in Law thus inevitably he would cultivate an interest in politics, joining the Ulster Unionist Party. Debate and challenge were his middle name, there was nothing he enjoyed more than someone having to eat their words. His very direct, loud opinion, N. Ireland was a sitting target for Germany.

Relative to the central topic of tailoring throughout this tale and giving a perfect illustration of the difficulties of mobilisation of small firms is the important shirt industry based in Derry city. It led the UK in this industry with the capacity of 30 firms fully equipped to produce clothing for the armed forces.

Collectively most of these firms employed less than 90 workers, yet they were largely unknown to the government and they found it impossible to agree on a common price. It is all ranks of organised confusion.

Miraculously by the spring of 1941 all of this disadvantage dissipated.

Contracts were won. The catalyst?

The shock response to the Belfast Blitz and the escalation of world conflict mixed with heightened awareness by both governments in Belfast and London of the urgency to recognise the industrial and manufacturing capacity of the workforce of N. Ireland.

The tables turned.

A little historical research reveals now that 14 firms were described as 'principal main contractors' engaged in war production inclusive of Harland and Wolff, Mackie's, Short and Harland and Combe Barbour. Names all greatly synonymous with N. Ireland.

They were significantly all based in County Antrim and County Down.

In textiles, 26 firms were main contractors for aeroplane linen, in the same counties bar ten which were contracted in County Armagh.

Derry/Londonderry had five out of seven principal main contractors for shirt manufacture for the army, navy and air force. While the two eastern counties dominated manufacture of serge battledress and denim suits.

So where were the Leopolds in the middle of all of this advocacy?

After all their workshop had since conception been manufacturing government clothing both in N. Ireland and England, in tandem with the bespoke tailoring. They made British Army uniforms of all calibres.

Surely they were not to be overlooked. There was a business to run, there were workers to be looked after, as father and son discussed the seriousness of their very existence.

Sonny could well understand his father's broken English, those in London certainly would not, so it was agreed Sonny was to do the talking, it only made sense.

The scene played out.

As was the norm for years in the running of business Sonny's job was sales; easy when the product you are selling is of a high quality and the production side of your business is run with the precision his father commanded. This meant he would have made regular trips to Bradford, England to buy material supplies, control individual deliveries and oversee larger shipments. Possessive of great social skills along with the rest, Sonny found himself in not only a position privy to military information but also in an influential political and social circle. It was not idle chat, it was debate and challenge.

Even before 1939 rumours abound of dangerous times ahead. The Leopolds trade saw themselves placed at the centre of many such conversations with more and more influential individuals. Then a friendship was struck up at this time with one of the most influential press barons in Britain, Lord Beaverbrook.

War was declared.

Events unfolded.

There was no time for hesitation, livelihoods were at stake. The Leopolds were ready, Sonny made the trip to England and personally presented their bid to extend production formally to the Ministry of Supply Office.

The Belfast workshop would begin manufacturing at full capacity from the outbreak of the conflict.

Within the first year of the war, 1940, Churchill appointed Lord Beaverbrook as Minister of Supply.

Sonny would take a call to immediately attend a meeting in London.

He was given an ultimatum.

"Get out of Belfast! Or lose the contract. Belfast is going to be bombed."

Back at the workshop Philip took his son's call.

"Dad, we have to get out of Belfast."

Father and son spoke with heavy hearts, forgiving each other for harsh words exchanged between them prior to Sonny making the trip. Philip, using the Jewish religious holiday to try and prevent him from travelling, when really his fear was the treacherous journey across the Irish Sea. One that he did not want his son to risk.

Speedily following orders, the Belfast Factory was boarded up. Sonny who had persistently raised concerns in heated words over the vulnerability of the harbour amongst other things would settle himself.

The machines, lock stock and barrel of the workshop were loaded up onto a convoy of lorries and transported out of the city.

The relocation was Dormore, County Down where two disused mills became home to the Leopolds. Here they set up dispersal factories working

24-hour shifts, seven days a week manufacturing British Army battle dress uniforms. Dangerous journeys over narrow roads, often at night during unavoidable blackout regulations with special permission in line with curfews.

Loyal staff signed up to the move.

This was no mean feat considering old habits die hard.

Not easy to convince the typical Belfast worker who was used to walking just a short distance to their workshop to get on a bus or train and travel sometimes upwards onto three hours. War or no war.

This problem was solved. Surely hard enough having to leave family, the staff made new homes when accommodation was provided and the townies began to live amongst their country compatriots. Travelling back to the big smoke after six day shifts on the buses or sometimes loaded into Sonny's car if he might have been travelling home at the same time.

It was no longer business as usual, Philip Leopold was 65 years old, no mention nor interest in retiring, relishing the challenge officially to play their part in the War Effort.

Sam Freeman would join them. In the atmosphere of xenophobia Philip's family, his tailors and his workforce remained loyal.

Sonny recalled, "You have no understanding of what tiredness is or indeed the hour of the day, knowing fine well the work has not stopped."

He watched his father never seem to take time to sleep even after a change of shifts, if he was not directing production, he was playing poker with senior staff, polishing off a bottle of whiskey, night after long night.

Listening to intermittent news bulletins crackling over the radio in their small corner office as workhouse machines whirred constantly in the background. Seems he was drowning out his grief. Thinking of his wife and maybe everything else.

His long-term workers knew the Boss nursed a sore heart, they were working hard for him, knowing he was for them.

Philip knew all about the lunacy of death and destruction, the psychopathy of war crimes, he escaped from it in another life and experienced the harrowing carnage brought by WWI, for those on the frontline in the military and those living in their home countries in the shadow of its terror.

He witnessed first-hand the aftermath of the Irish famine, the Irish Rebellion and Partition of Ireland 1922, holding tight for family onto the vast successful industrialisation of the North.

It would always be about stretching for harmony before aggression and for survival it was about being fit to recognize the silver lining in the clouds.

What now? As a new sales counter stretched across the rear of the drapers shop.

For why? The lads at the barricades needed plastic buckets and plenty of them. Boulders, bricks, sticks and worse.

"Are you a Protestant Jew or a Catholic Jew?" Was the call of the wild.

"Just a Jew." Sonny would naively quip, all ten years of age. As father and son serviced the needs of their warring neighbours. Negotiating skills were born in the midst of the dangerous 1920's. There were bigger stakes at risk come the 1940's.

THE FREEMANS HELL

Sam and Bea's son Lesley attended Belfast Royal Academy, he was a charming young boy, full of fun, loving life, loving school life and loving rugby as he hit his teenage years. Of course they had expectations. Why not?

Then time stood still, the cast of misfortune came into play and as a result of a knock on the field cancer struck and his health spiralled out of control.

1941 Christmas Day. Despite frantic efforts to find a cure, no stone left unturned, Leslie, their shining light, died aged 18.

Beryl was ten years old when the policeman who stood uncomfortably on the doorstep of their terrace home on the Bank Road in Larne, straightened himself to muster his composure and then he delivered the tragic news. Her father Tommy bore the news to Neska but could see the anguish in his daughter's face as she came down the stairs, shaking her head beseeching him to say it was not true.

It could not be true. After all she cried, Leslie had just smiled into her face as she lay on her bed.

In this darkness Bea and Sam would not attend their son's funeral, they had not yet recovered from the death of their daughter one year earlier 1940, 28th December.

Everything hurt them, they could not find solace, only in each other.

So it was to be as the family made their way up to the Jewish cemetery.

In the midst of war supporting each other, the vicious cold breeze of winter on the slopes of Carnmoney overlooking Belfast, cut into them without mercy.

It fell to the grandfather to bury his grandson.

Leslie was then laid to rest in front of his sister and beside his grandmother, with a grave between them for his grandfather eventually.

LESLIE

I'm crying my son can you hear me
The lights have gone out, I cannot see
Grief has weakened me, it has to be said
I can't breathe, for, in this moment.
I too am dead

– Geraldine Connon

1941 THE SEQUENCE AND ESCALATION OF THE WAR MACHINE IN THE UK, NORTHERN IRELAND AND USA

My memory recounts the teaching of my history teacher at Larne Grammar School, Mr Michael Lawson, who had his own stories to relay about the war. Mr Lawson's father was head of the Fleet Street spin team of journalists brought out of retirement in WWII, to write copy to keep readers' spirits buoyant in response to radio reports of the war and likewise confuse the enemy that they were not winning. Michael of course does not remember one occasion, which shows the attempts made then to have a certain normality in life. His christening, celebrated in the newspaper offices where his father worked with his colleagues. Meanwhile.

APRIL: After the Belfast Blitz, the UK War Department held secret talks for six months with their American elite military counterparts. Resulting in the issue of the RAINBOW 5 plan which envisioned wartime deployment of 87,000 American troops to the United Kingdom.

Approximately 30,000 of the troops are to be based in N. Ireland.

Even at this stage the general public opinion amongst American citizens was not to enter the war.

My history notes, yes I too have saved school jotters.

7 DECEMBER: Japanese forces attack with ferocity and stealth American relatively undefended military might at Pearl Harbour. Almost the entire Pacific Fleet was moored around Ford Island in the harbour and hundreds of airplanes were squeezed onto adjacent airfields. The Japanese saw Pearl Harbour as an irresistible easy target.

8 DECEMBER: USA declares war on Japan and enters WWII.

17 DECEMBER: After 5 independent visits and reports to the region MG Chaney submits a written report on his review of the situation following American entry into the war, and specifically in reference to the existing plan to send 33,421 American troops to N. Ireland. His report concludes that contracts still need to be let for housing for 9,703 personnel.

That became the significant immediate urgency.

In plain language, where was this influx of manpower going to live?

In the end an estimated 300,000 Americans would move into Northern Ireland from the beginning of 1942, taking up residence until the end of the war. Approximately one tenth of the Province's population and a significant upsurge in male rank and file.

Private estates, hotels, castles, farms and public buildings were requisitioned for accommodation needs. Tentage was plentiful and thousands of Nissan huts were built every day in the luscious green countryside and in the grounds of the majority of these properties.

Country lanes were swimming with GIs. The city and towns Province wide virtually inherited a small nation and culture of military men.

By 31st May 1942, most of the U.S. Army ground forces in the British Isles were in N. Ireland, leaving it the sole garrisoned area under the title USANIF (United States of America Northern Ireland Force). Within the time frame of the next year.

Meanwhile civilians lived in an atmosphere of fear and anxiety of the unknown. Curfew and rations, in new enforced work environments alongside unemployment and poverty as well as homelessness in many cases, listening to and reading media reports daily of death and conflict on the military front and witnessing the return to home of mentally and physically broken men and women. Families decimated by the loss of loved ones came to truly value small tokens of kindness and generosity of their neighbours and then the American military arrived bringing a renewed confidence that the Allies would win the war as well as an element of financial affluence. Two very different cultures would cohabit this island for four years, following the well documented two rules of conduct for the American abroad,

'Don't argue religion. Don't argue politics.'

The American speak was quite different to that of the British army and very much that of the typical N. Irish, a confidence in themselves as being the saviours of the day. This would lift the spirits of their new found neighbours but these young men and women were no different to those of other nations when it came to the battlefields and final insurmountable global death tally.

Poignantly from the sanctity of Northern Ireland having been immersed in our culture in preparation for their deployment, the skies usually at nightfall over isolated countryside, small towns, harbours and villages would carry the haunting voices of young American soldiers and their commanding officers singing melodies of the Irish ballads, 'Sweet Molly Malone', 'It's a Long Way to Tipperary', even 'The Fields of Athenry'.

On the dawning of the next day, they would all be gone to war.

THE WAR AS IT PROGRESSED

Selective News Headlines

Remarkably N. Ireland, its location, citizens and workforce would be of extraordinary importance, not only to Great Britain but also to the United States.

By 1942 the Province was fully immersed in the war effort as news from Europe would filter in mostly through radio broadcasts, editorials and cinema announcements.

That year reports covered Germany's setbacks at Stalingrad and El Alamein, Japanese successes in Singapore and an American naval victory at the Battle of Midway in June, marking a turning point in the Pacific.

What failed to be reported on was the onslaught of mass murder of Jewish people in Auschwitz concentration camp. The extent of the death-camps only coming to light at the end of the war. Operation Reinhard (1942–43) being the largest single murder campaign of the Holocaust which would leave 1.7 million innocent Jews dead.

British Intelligence was aware that the vitriolic murderous assault of the race had already started in 1939.

Prime Minister Winston Churchill summarised events in a broadcast to the public in 1941. A man who could say a few words with far reaching clarity.

1942: In the spring when the United States entered the war, Glen Stadler UP (United Press) correspondent in Germany described what was happening to the Jews as that of animals being hunted.

1942: 13th December.

With reference to Edward R, Murrow of CBS radio network, he bluntly reported the ruthless efficiency in which Jews were being murdered in their millions. He would call it extermination.

Hitler, his elite commandants and his army were demonically out of control.

One of the most horrific terms in history was born in Germany at that time

LEBENSUNWERTES LEBEN or LIFE UNWORTHY OF LIFE

The Nazi policy to murder civilians en masse, later growing into the Fuhrer's FINAL SOLUTION, the complete extermination of Jews.

In 1942, no one was sure of what the outcome would be. Appalling atrocities would continue, man's inhumanity to man saw no boundaries.

BELFAST AND DROMORE

Ordinary people everywhere had to adapt to change. Chance, luck and circumstance dictated the outcome. Back in Belfast and now in Dromore, Leopold battledress manufacture continued with staff well used to their new life norm in the midst of war. Even in adversity, curfew, death or misplacement, resilience existed, humour, even dark humour lightened conversation. So, work was different, at least it was work. Rationing was hard, sure did you not know someone who would smuggle you butter or chocolate over the border, what about the GIs? They can get any amount of silk stockings. People who were grateful for small mercies, themselves not on the frontline, yet supporting those living still in fear of family who were. So the Northern Irish knuckled down.

The girls in the Leopold factories in Dormore would soon have a new topic of conversation. Even in these dark days there would still have been the odd spark of good news. Who would have thought it would be Sonny of all people, who would cause a stir and most definitely lighten gossip on the machines.

As with most confirmed bachelors, despite their best efforts, they let their guard down, cupid's bow strikes and they eventually fall in love.

On a trip to England for business Sonny's path crossed that of petite Phyllis Freedman who hailed from Newcastle upon Tyne. Phyllis was the PA to an officer in the British army and caught Sonny's eye as he was delivering a couple of bespoke uniforms. He WAS caught.

This artistic lass was ever so slightly eccentric and amusing, added to that fact she had the most striking looks. For God's sake, how could Sonny resist her. A long-distance romance was struck up and their love affair blossomed.

1944 15th October, they were married in Belfast.

1945 2nd SEPTEMBER

Then finally it was over, the war that is, the world wept and cheered simultaneously.

That elation would be very short lived as the utter extent of the carnage was laid bare. The cruel massacres never before witnessed or matched on such a catastrophic global scale affected millions of people worldwide.

In 1918 it had been thought possible at the end of the first world war that business could return as usual, in 1945 that could never have been a consideration, so much so that it was to be called 'Year Zero'.

1945 KRIUKAI LITHUANIA

The paths the Lepars walked for better, for worse.

In the immediate years from when Philip had first left, his elder brother Shmuel had made his bid for freedom from the Empire also. So driven was he that he walked overland to Palestine only to be captured by the British army and returned to Kriukai. That did not deter him as once he had regained his strength he walked it again, joining in the battle for the birth of Israel and claiming his right to live there. He too would never look back.

Shmuel when it came to his turn met his sweetheart in Israel. Their life was decided as they settled there and would welcome their own son Nachum.

So the remaining Lepars lived out their lives in the Pale close to their community. How they survived the relentless, brutal persecution of Jews beggar's belief. Yet they did, through the Russian Revolution in 1917, and WWI. Younger members would breathe fresh life into the family and new ambitions for travel and destination were awakened when in 1931 Michael's daughter Luba married and immigrated to Costa Rica. She in turn would then bring her sister Fanny and brother Max over to join them. On the outbreak of war despite their religion it was this move which saved their lives, the question was, would the remaining family weather this storm?

Cast your thoughts wildly and imagine abject fear.

As telegrams wired world wide of allied victories, they were laced with all kind of news. In Belfast and Dublin few desolating words.

Blood ran cold.

Michael the eldest Lepar brother, without a blessing and no such right to an honourable burial along with the remaining 15 members of the family including Alec's father Barry were to witness and face the unthinkable. As they locked down in their family compound, truly hopeful their neighbours would defend them, surely for pity's sake, unaware like so many million others that their fate was sealed they cautiously were living out their final days.

Even in their isolated rural surroundings, the Nazis sympathisers, grappling with no conscience, levied their grotesque insanity on the extended Lepar family.

Within six months of entering WWII, the USA invaded Russia in 1942, believed to be the catalyst in triggering the Lithuanian Holocaust.

Yet the previous year, simmering antisemitism ever present, gathered pace under the leadership of Col. Kazys Skirpa, the Lithuanian ambassador to Germany. As he took control of the Leituvij Frontas (the Lithuanain Activist Front or LAF), composed of far right and centre political groups and police units, his encouragement and direction of Nazi ideology and racist concepts were unleashed.

Even before the German troops reached the principal murder sites of Kaunas, Vilnius and Siauliai and before Juozas Ambraze Vicius and leaders of the LAF established a Provisional Government, the purpose of which was to establish an 'independent Lithuanian state' as an ally of Nazi Germany.

As the last week of June 1941 unfolded, massacres began. The most notorious and well documented carried out by Lithuanian elements, armed with iron bars and wooden clubs.

Rabbi Ossouski was beheaded by army officer Vitkauskas and his head prominently displayed from the upstairs window of the Lietukis Garage in Kaunas. It was all barbaric.

1941 26th June: all the Jews in Kriukai and surrounding towns were rounded up by Lithuanian 'activist' units and concentrated in a ghetto in the nearby centre of Zagare.

On Yom Kippur, thousands of Jewish men, women and children were moved out of town, the Lepars amongst them, rounded off from their land and property, verbally abused by their accusers and marched for a mile or so into the neighbouring Zagare Forest. All of them executed, shot in the head into mass open graves.

Who amongst them would have watched the others death play out systematically until it was their turn?

The last communication received – sent before the Nazi invasion – from Michael to Fanny, Max and Luba read, "We have nothing to fear from our German business friends."

By the time the letter arrived in Costa Rica they had all been killed by their own countrymen.

The tears from Central America would reach N. Ireland.

The brutality of it stripped the Belfast tailors of any peace of mind.

The task of running two factories, furnishing major government contracts took its toll. The pressure would have been fierce, on top of which there had been no guarantee since 1939 that the allies would win the war.

Then when it was all over and victory for freedom was declared, could it be deemed possible they would claim their lives back. Spirits had been raised, could they contemplate peace at last?

Then the telegrams began to arrive in Belfast. They were from official sources read in disbelief with the understanding it was all true.

Philip wept openly as his family watched on, his heart and mind helplessly turned to Kriukai. Everyone left belonging to him and Alec was gone. He would have been in Hell, Hell on earth, imagining their fear, their pain, their final moments. All gone.

Now in this year 2021, a new book has reached the book stands.

The Nazi's Granddaughter by Silvia Foti.

Upon making a promise to her mother on her deathbed to recount the tale of her father Jonas Noreika, Silvia who had been reared to believe her grandfather was a WWII military hero discovered in her own words that he was in fact a monster responsible for the annihilation of the Jewish population throughout the region of Siauliai, Plunge and Kriukai researched to the exact date of 1941. Silvia is very poignant and deliberate in revealing her findings and in her address to the families of those who were exterminated she offers her deepest apologies, knowing forgiveness cannot be an option as only the murdered can forgive.

Michael's granddaughter Guita made that pilgrimage to Lithuania to find the family home, to speak to residents to find answers. She filmed all she could with futile answers.

LOS LABERINTOS DE LA MEMORIA

A documentary film by GUITA SCHYFTER

Researching the village and final days of the Lepar family in Kriukai.

30th April 1945 Adolf Hitler along with his wife of one day Eva Braun retreated to the bunker under the Chancellery in Berlin, 55 feet down towards hell, poisioned his alsatian dog Blondi and committed suicide.

Russian FSB secret service and the Russian State archives would give permission in 2018 for skull fragments and bits of teeth to be examined confirming the memoirs of a Russian interpreter who had been entrusted with his teeth in 1945. Today they remain in Russian hands. Hold that celebratory date close because within only fourteen years.

30th April 1959 Beryl and Gerry Connon welcome their daughter Geraldine into this world.

THE CATHOLIC, THE PROTESTANT, THE BLACK, THE JEW THE MUSLIM, THE ATHEIST, THE IMMIGRANT AND THEN YOU

What value have these beings, anywhere?
Their existence is futile, worthless and bare
What do they offer? Nothing just nothing I can see
For I am superior Look at me Look at me
Be careful, stay awake, watch your mind
For I am sinister, sinful and selfishly not kind
Woe betide I take hold of your voice
For I will own you, everything will be my choice
Said the King of demonic jealousy and greed
to the Prince of paupers weakened by need

– Geraldine Connon

Philip became intensely unwell. Brought to his knees with a severe heart attack. No longer invincible and suddenly now a 70 year old man.

Yet and yet I stress he fought back as war came to an end.

When the first losses compounded by 1941, Sam and Philip consoled each other in their grief. Their work had offered them some solace, in fact the frantic workload of the military uniform contract helped.

Philip had mad courage, more than most. Perhaps it was easier for him to fill his day with work than give into emotion, perhaps in lone moments as he slowly recovered his health, he gave into it. Yet as the family stood round him, he in turn would stand his ground as the father even in his weakness. Stop the fussing, stop the crying, straighten up.

A big move was announced, the newlyweds, Sonny and Phyll (as she was affectionately called) moved into their own home, Kelvin Parade, only a street away. So as with tradition the ever-growing Belfast family stayed close by each other all still working under the umbrella of the tailoring house and all concerned to protect one another, a reason for Sam and Bea to move in with them under their roof.

Soon, excitement lifted them all when the first son was born. He would be called Leslie, named after his cousin who had died three years earlier on Christmas day and then Marshall was born. Two boys of very different temperaments. It had been hoped that the babies would help soothe the loss of the young cousins for their parents yet it brought its own mixture of harrowing memories for the children, especially Leslie.

To this day he can recall hearing his aunt crying inconsolably for her own, as a child not understanding for why. Then his mind happily remembers with great joy his uncle Sam taking him to the cinema most Saturday afternoons. As shows the impressionable minds of children, how would they possibly understand the impact of death.

Bea would gather herself too as her sisters supported her in her loss, sharing their own daughters with her. Nevertheless how would innocently childish Bea ever recover? It was Sam who faithfully comforted his wife talking and forever talking quietly as they held each other every night.

The Freemans chose to embrace their nieces and nephews as they began to socialise. Sam for his part would regularly hire a box at the Opera House, hire a taxi for him and the family brood to add to the experience and drive into the City. What pleasure that brought them all.

Watching the children's expressions during a performance such as Cinderella, saw his heart and spirit sing to their wide eyed gazes.

Bea for her part loved to dine out. Beryl and she enjoyed many visits to the most famous hotel in Ireland back then, the Grand Central Hotel on Royal Avenue before it was commissioned for the war machine and stripped of its grandeur; all because of a misdirected letter meant for the Grand Central in Birmingham. Still, Bea had already introduced her niece to the luxury. Afternoon tea, the most favourite outing. Leading the way she loved to escort her young niece through the reception into the dining room, choose a suitable table for them and once comfortably seated, place their order, coffee for her, tea for Beryl. The memory Beryl would forever recall, "Auntie Bea always held her little finger out when she drank from her china cup."

Funny she would end up with the exact trait herself. Bea quietly wanted her nieces to learn by example. So her sister married out, that was her choice, it was deemed as such an act of betrayal of the faith at the time.

Bea personally had more love than most to share.

Despite the deed, the home would always be sacred.

Neska never left her family, they never left her.

At times they would have lost patience with each other, certainly not with any of the children.

Eventually Sam and Bea would become stronger and move into their own flat still near everyone.

This gave Sonny and Phyll and their two boys their home to themselves, if only for a short time.

Close by in Harry Cohen's home, Dolly had never quite had enough time to come to terms with losing her mother, then there were the deaths of Dorothy and Leslie along with watching Dada suffer so much as a consequence of the murders in Russia.

Mistakenly thinking all of this was stripping her of her energy. She and Harry were occupied with their own children yet she could not shake off what she thought was sadness. Just seeing her father broken, killed her peace, yet her two daughters brought such love and pride. Two girls for her to dress up. Maybe even follow in her footsteps. How long she kept her weakness to herself only she knows, eventually she would seek medical advice.

The diagnosis was tragic.

For Dolly it was to be fatal, her beautiful looks cruelly savaged.

Despite all efforts nothing could save her.

As her final days broke the resolve of everyone, unable to watch her suffering, it was Beryl's father Tommy who sat with her in hospital. Holding a cup for her as she took tiny sips of tea.

One bittersweet memory from that sad time stayed with him. On opening her eyes Dolly every now and then would have said,

"Oh Tommy, am I still here? I was in such a beautiful place! "

Tragically within the year Harry Cohen died as well, a dreadful turn of fate leaving their girls with no parents. Their pitiful young cries echoed around the rooms of their grandfather's house where they first stayed after the funeral. Sonny and Phyll once again would offer solace under their roof. Phyll showered the girls with kindness, love and care, so much more her beautiful spirit and delight to do than bothersome housework.

Be Still These Broken Hearts.

1946 BELFAST LEOPOLD HOUSEHOLD

Summer Holidays After the War Years as recounted by Beryl

So a new era begins.

Following a lifetime in the rag trade and all that it brought, emotions were frayed as inevitably Philip calmed himself knowing it was a new life now for all of them.

The roles were somewhat reversed.

Four seasons came and went and the Leopolds regained some energy, the grandchildren were now mostly teenagers except for Sonny and Phyllis's two boys and they were good company. Philip had let go of work and had begun to enjoy the fruits of his hard-earned labour.

Although the family had always spent time together now Dada had more free time too.

From 1946 onwards the extended Leopolds holidayed for a month in the summer in numerous locations both North and South of the border.

Beryl could enjoy the best of two worlds, her Jewish family in Belfast and her Catholic family in Fermanagh while the first ventured to the resorts, the latter drew her mostly to Carnboy and the family home, grandma Rolston preferring everyone to stay close to her.

As the official celebrations marking the end of the war took place in towns throughout the country it gave the triumphant returning regiments the glory of their victory parade, marching to the sound of military bands and applause of their civilian families, neighbours and friends.

The long road to social and economic recovery then had to commence.

Precipitous decisions, protocol and red tape.

Despite numerous official orders for the destruction of surplus equipment which sadly could have been salvaged, the UK government did amongst other things come to an arrangement and purchased hundreds of Nissan huts aware of the lack of social housing in the wider community in built up areas of the North.

Initially it was a relief, nearly an adventure for families to find themselves housed in these ex-military huts. That war spirit would live on for a considerable time in line with fourteen years of food rationing that only ended on 4th July 1954, nine years after the end of the war.

However as modern council housing was established in N. Ireland the lifespan of temporary accommodation would cease. This would not follow throughout the Province when particular communities found themselves still living in by now the poorly maintained, rundown council owned structures with no modern facilities.

In some cases decades later there was a deep sense of inequality and unhappiness amongst these neighbourhoods, meanwhile in Fermanagh this would not be the case for Tommy Rolston's sister Sissy in the countryside of Lisnarick. Pat Murphy, her husband, was delighted to purchase a Nissan hut and rebuild it nestled amongst trees on her family's small landholding. He then set about converting it into the most beautiful home for them complete with maple wood floors throughout, partitioned living, dining and bedrooms through to the most important room for Sissy, her kitchen. They then filled it with an eclectic mix of antique furniture, china, linens, drapes even cutlery all salvaged from large houses in the area whose residents sold them on the side of the road eager to clear old furniture from their houses in favour of the new wave of modern furniture sweeping the country side in the 1950s.

So inviting was this home that my sister and I, even though we were very young when we visited with mum and dad, remember the beauty and the aromatic warmth of it along with the perfectly dressed dining table and Auntie Sissy's homemade bread and jam.

Sissy and Pat, just like Tommy, loved gardening, never too anxious about forcing plants to grow, letting nature and wildlife seed their garden for them. Gardening would be Tommy's hobby at home on the Bank Road, winning him awards in local competitions and even on one very fine day an anonymous letter with £20 inside it was left to congratulate him on his beautifully tidy rows of onions. That was a tale for the Fermanagh ones.

Any wonder the Larne Rolstons were drawn down to Carnboy.

Any wonder when they had to leave as grandma sat on her chair in the middle of her kitchen waiting for the goodbye kisses, Tommy would quietly say, "Now run in and give her a quick kiss and remember no crying." Meanwhile Uncle George would have already disappeared up through the fields, no goodbyes for him.

As it so happened Donegal was to be the joint favourite location for all the extended family, Bundoran in particular saw visits from the Catholics and the Jews.

Yet it was Glenties which held the greatest favour for Philip. A place he had discovered even before the partition of Ireland. Simply greatly facilitated by the far-reaching rail network the country boasted of a hundred years ago. He and Rose along with close business friends would holiday there taking such solace in the natural terrain of the locality with its great similarities to their home in Russia.

Symbolized by the Yiddish saying, Alla Schwartz Yoren. Literally meaning 'All the black years', but as with Yiddish the meaning changed holding a dual interpretation and significance.

Perfectly describing the Donegal of the day as 'The back of beyond', and at the same time recognising the Jewish people's way of not looking to the dark past. Donegal, the Fort of Foreigners.

As far back as the 1920s Philip invested in his own car, a rarity of the times and the family found themselves holidaying in Bray, County Wicklow or sometimes Newcastle and Portrush. Dada would hire a summer house for whomever wanted to come, always wanting family around him. A growing family with all the passing years.

Making great friends leaving a trail of Jewishness behind them.

Of course Philip loved these trips, the biggest draw being his favourite photographic studio on the promenade. He was their best customer. When Beryl and her cousin Gloria went to meet him there on one occasion they stood in awe, smiling at each other with humour because the photographer in his wisdom had adorned all the walls with their grandfather's portraits.

So who is Gloria? Well she is only another granddaughter of Philip's.

NESKA'S SISTER PEGGY [HIKA] LEOPOLD

Fifth in line of the children Peggy was born in 1906. That would mean five girls in six years. The parents were keeping their pact with each day more and more proud of their growing brood of young ladies.

Peggy would not let them down. She too would be an attention stealer, fair of face with beautiful fine features as early family photographs clearly portray. The Leopolds had their hands full. Halfway there.

The daily home routine would be polished by this time as these girls grew up, it was only as they found their feet as teenagers that they were uncontrollable. Sadly so spoiled and naive that they would always be provided for. Life would never turn on them. No such possibility.

In the 1920s the workshop yet again would not fail.

Much as she loved style embracing any and every excuse to dress up Peggy too would never be destined to join the family firm. All the same she was more than happy to frequent the workshop in her teens. The reason would soon become apparent as she found true love with another employee of her father's, a gentleman who worked on the cutting floor, quiet amiable Mac (Michael) Gould. It was quite inevitable.

Mac had another string to his bow, he was a drummer in a show band.

More than exciting to Peggy, introducing her to a glamorous nightlife which her parents would never have permitted only for Mac. Eventually opportunity arose for him in the entertainment scene and the two of them once they got married, upped sticks from Belfast and moved into a luxurious apartment in Dublin.

Peggy was in her element, too beautiful for her own good as she joined the fashion set, finding Mac's sister a catwalk model, the perfect lady friend to lunch with. Soft kiss curls across her forehead framing her angelic face, dressed in the latest always, Peggy could easily compete.

Eventually she and Mac would have a daughter and that was Gloria.

Gloria Gould, the absolute centre of her parent's world.

Peggy lost herself because for her Gloria was everything, hardly allowed to look out of her own eyes, except that is when she joined her cousins, aunts, uncles and her Granda on the annual holidays.

Beryl and she were firm friends for those few weeks as they enjoyed a little bit of freedom from the usual form of being seen not heard.

Nervous teenage years would come and go and then following her mother's lead Peggy and Gloria could swan into a room with the grace worthy of film actresses.

Gloria hit the social scene in Dublin fit for all the attention not just for her looks but her beguiling singing voice winning her an array of eligible admirers with her party piece, the love song 'Besame Mucho'. The right one would make his move, little did she know her mother would never be able to let go of her.

Peggy loved Gloria too much. The siblings knew she lived in the clouds yet all of them suffered from that other vice, believing money grew on trees. They, way back then, chased the rule of our time, the 'Bank of dad'.

"Why can't you speak out like Gloria?" Neska would have lamented to Beryl wanting her daughter to come out of the shadows.

That was never Beryl's way and sadly Gloria and she lost contact.

Nothing escaped Philip's watchful eye. He loved his quiet granddaughter's manner, forever fussing over her when she and her mum travelled up on the train from Larne once a week to spend the day. That was the sisters catch up time, the gossip and drama of the week, their theatrics worthy of the stage and when dinner was served, in the midst of it all, he made sure Beryl sat beside him, insisting as Grandas do, no matter what was on her plate, he had to share his food with her.

Always.

Back in Donegal, the holiday antics continued.

Many locals had become friends over the years, looking forward to the summer season and the visit from the Belfast Jews.

Hoteliers, Dawson's Amusement Arcade, Benuglies Ice Cream Parlor, as well as the photographers' studios all welcomed the Leopolds.

Honorary members of their unsolicited card school, the not-so-secret gamblers willing to play poker well into the wee hours indulging in the odd brandy or two. That was the routine.

Now the work arena was over, the boss, Philip had earned his well-deserved peace at last. He could enjoy it, he could play the game, yet his portrait, still handsome as he was, could not mask his heartache.

Funnily enough he was always the consummate tailor. Retaining his opinions naturally and offering them freely without fear of recourse from the recipient. Not remotely believing that he could possibly be offending them.

He would frequently remark on people's clothes, feeling the cloth of a gentleman's jacket in passing and in a few words tell them,

"Not good, Not good!"

His daughter Millie always worried about what people thought, would have interjected the conversation regularly and whispered under her breath,

"Dada why do you have to let everyone know that you are a tailor?"

Reminds me of a lady who used to work for me and who efficiently brushed off any threads from her clothes so people would think, in her words, that she was a secretary not a stitcher. Dear Kathleen from the Shankill Road, Belfast, who jokingly recalled how her soon to be husband said every time he opened his front door she was standing there with her suitcase.

Poor Millie, not only had to watch her fathers' chat, Albert and she would not escape his daughters' honesty and innocence either.

A couple of summers in a row whilst residing in Molloys Hotel the Leopolds found themselves sharing the same floor as a distinguished English couple. Captain Benson and his wife made the yearly trip to Ireland for the fishing season followed up by the Dublin Horse Show.

Rose and Beryl shared the bedroom adjacent to Mrs Benson's room, where her jet black labrador slept outside the door. As was the norm, Captain Benson dressed in a green silk night shirt and floppy nightcap appeared from his room down the corridor to say goodnight and turn the landing light off.

Smiling to himself, on one occasion as he recalled the enthusiasm of Rose earlier in the day when she had told him that her daddy fished as well and produced Albert's glorious makeshift line and hook from behind his seat.

"Well sure , if it does the job." he had graciously agreed.

On the same holiday both Millie and Albert joined forces to distract attention when the Bensons niece arrived with a flurry of excitement amongst all the hotel residents in the knowledge she had been a guest at the present day Queen's (Beryl's words) engagement party.

Being as her dress sense followed the country style of a fairisle sweater and tweed skirt. Mr Leopold senior and his two granddaughters adopted a nod and wink in public as a matter of manners under Millie's fixed glare.

1947 BERYL'S MEMOIRES KINGSMERE AVENUE BELFAST

Beryl, sweet 16, started work in fashion retail in Belfast, moving from sales into window dressing. A job she was cut out for, enlivening surroundings far removed from her quiet hometown of Larne.

A few years earlier as it turned out her parents had agreed that she could attend ballroom dancing classes with close neighbours. There she met her lifelong friend Gladys Meneely and it was these two young damsels who became travelling companions on the daily train commute to Belfast. So as life was opening up she began to innocently enjoy her youth and freedom.

The city pace suited her, the shops, her co-workers, darting on and off trams and darting passed the street photographers who seemed to catch her and Gladys at every chance.

The girls secured jobs in adjacent ladies fashion shops in the city centre, Gladys in McMahon's milliners, employment which required her to wear a hat to work, something which she only unrolled out of her coat pocket and adorned in the hallway before she walked over the doorstep, Beryl in McWilliams and Archers, a Ladies Fashion shop, run somewhat in the style of the fictional department store Grace Brothers the TV series *Are You Being Served*.

Those were the days of protocol. But there was always humour to be had more so amongst the junior staff. The man in charge happened to be Jewish, Davy Danker, a bit of a perfectionist, highly strung and run on a short fuse. There are many stories to be told from the shop, a couple do stand out. As Beryl assisted Mr Danker dressing the windows, a common request of his was frequently, "A pin Miss Rolston," and should there have been even a slight delay, his tone would have become an increasingly high pitched shrill, "A pin, a pin, a pin, a pin."

This of course became a great source of amusement and to heighten the hysterics Beryl's favourite co-worker Lilly Mc Donald would often stand behind him poised with a pin ready to prick him. Other friends who worked in the city would often pass by the window on such days and beckon to Beryl from the footpath as they imitated with hilarity, her boss behind his back, gesturing a little bit this way and a little bit the other.

Davy wanted sales, he understood the value of presentation, the shop layout, the stock and of course the greatest platform for sales, the shop windows. To watch him was an education in his successes and even in his PR disasters.

His most outlandish purchase took centre stage as Beryl and he dressed the shop's main window for one particular autumn/winter season. Surrounded by the latest accessories there on display adorning the main mannequin was the jaw droppingly, god awful bright red wool coat with an oversized black velvet bow fixed at the waist, painstakingly turned in place for passers-by to get the full benefit of it.

Davy, quite enamoured with his choices, waltzed and swooned around the shop in glory.

The staff silently flashed knowing looks between them, understanding their opinion was not to be given. In this fresh atmosphere on the shop-floor, it just had to be Beryl who greeted a couple of new customers. Belfast Townies well renowned for their wit.

"So ladies, how can I be of help?"

"Well Miss any chance we could try that coat in the window on? Just for the gegg!!!!" Hey wee girl, are you from Belfast?

Get out of that one I dare you, Beryl could hear Lilly's thoughts from behind her counter.

Take the coat out of the display knowing it was never to be a sale, I don't think so. Beryl, by this time in her training had the answer,

"Sorry ladies, that coat is not for sale, it is purely for display."

As the highly amused duo tried in vain to coax her.

Yet on another occasion when Beryl transferred jobs to Barnett Hutton's, embracing the rule of the day that the customer is always right she would indeed struggle to please a customer. Attending to her every whim as she posed from mirror to mirror in coat after coat or dress after dress. It was only when her new boss, Mr Goodson, came to the door of his office from where he had been watching the performance and called her to him.

"Suzy," as he named her, flustered and walking towards him only to hear him say under his breath. "Throw her out."

This lady for those that know the score was killing time. Dare I suggest that the customer is not always right For the most of it, Beryl loved working in the city, back then she felt the world was her oyster. Just as the majority of 19-year-olds do, isn't that so?

One of the greatest pleasures of the week was to visit her grandfather every Monday evening. As she recounts, she just shouted hello as she came in through the front door and then ran up the stairs to sit with him for a very precious hour, chatting freely about anything and everything. How poignant this time would have been for Philip accepting of his age and sadly his fragility, how was he going to protect her forever?

Inevitably when she was saying her goodbyes, he would tap his forehead waiting for her goodbye kiss. In effect all of his grandchildren would visit him, they all had their own time with him and so looked forward to their money present hidden in his bedside cabinet, their spending power for the week. He enjoyed being their defender watching his fiery daughters and son watching their every move. Never feeling he had to lay the law down with them, the younger generation.

Beryl and her cousins knew their place yet always granda Philip amused them with his antics. Secretly buying them jewellery, hiding their forbidden cigarettes, attempting to use curse words, his most prolific phrase being:

"Yu are a stick-ass" claiming it was " a wery wery bad verd ".

They also loved his feckless attempts to bluff whilst playing five-card draw poker, a customary evening's entertainment. Dominoes, poker and boxing the order of the day or night as it happens.

Boxing being his greatest love, catching the tram at the top of the Cliftonville Road, he and whoever was free of an evening would attend matches in the city centre at every opportunity.

"Who is fighting tonight, Granda?"

Beryl asked as she joined him, Bea and Albert and Millie on the tram down onto York Street to get her train home.

"Rinty Monaghan" was the answer, the undisputed World Flyweight Champion 1947–50. It was Rinty who had everyone talking. The local lad, a hero of Belfast and the cause of such excitement and anticipation.

Philip backed him all the way, he encouraged and applauded the fighting spirit of young boxers. Even from the 1920s regardless of deadlines there was always time for a bit of rivalry between the message boys when they called at his workshop Philip had boxing gloves to hand. They looked forward to the challenge and break in their day, never mind the winner's fee. It was the era when boxing was deemed the sport of kings however the most marvellous thing was in this ring being poor had the edge. That appeal resonated amongst the working class, a sport available to the bravest.

Belfast as it turns out was home to many fist fighters back in the day. The fighter did not need money, he needed strength, unyielding spirit and grit to be that title holder.

LIFE ALWAYS MOVES ON

Despite passions whether it was boxing, entertainment, holidays, food, the topic of fashion was the all-consuming debate, unlikely to be beaten.

As the ensuing years passed, time as we know it too is the great healer.

There was youth in the family now breathing freshness to everyone.

The sun would shine again on them. Who would bring that to the home?

Well it was Dolly and Harry's eldest daughter.

Gladys, all grown up, started dating. There were plenty of suitable young Jewish men and when the time was right a match was made and she got engaged to Percy Silverstein. The family were ready to celebrate and once again everyone had something to look forward to.

Philip, a changed man, older and quite frail if he would have admitted it, stepped up to the mark. Childishly relishing his latest role, charged with walking his granddaughter down the aisle. He could hardly contain his pleasure at the thought of it. Preparations commenced and there was such a flurry of excitement.

Everyone played their part. Dada was no different than the rest of them. He was also walking on a cane, albeit a beautiful cane. Anyhow he would most definitely not be using it. Ignoring the consternation and arguments put to him.

At every opportunity he would walk up and down the hall of his home, rehearsing. Glancing in the mirror this elderly gentleman could only see a strong man. Straightening his shoulders, his mind took him back in time. The years disappeared and he, as he walked forward, only saw himself on his own wedding day. Strong and virile, humble but proud. Then she appeared at his side, softly smiling at him, the vision of Rose his beloved Rose. Smiling back at her he placed his hand on his heart as if to hold her. Willing her spirit to be with him. If only she had lived just a little while longer to fully enjoy what he had most loved and wanted for her and their family. Their beautiful house on a tree lined Avenue as Kingsmere was.

He could imagine her arm resting though his, he could remember her touch on his hand and he could remember her perfume.

Philip needed to make it real so knowing she would yield willingly to his requests Beryl stepped in as the pretend bride.

Linking his granddaughter his confidence grew, the cane was most certainly not required. That was but for one exception. He would have to make sure Gladys had shoes she could walk in. As was the weakness of the Leopold females. On one occasion as he and Beryl practised the walk up the hall she wobbled ungainly in her shoes and he exclaimed, "For vye you wear those shoes, for vye?"

"They are style Grandad," she replied as he shook his head in dismay.

What's with the shoes in this family? Dada treated all his girls to bespoke dresses from Mrs Glazier's Elite Dressmakers Fashion House by the City Hall in Belfast. Once again wedding fever took them over.

Quietly keeping her thoughts to herself never once mentioning it, Neska, of all of them, never got the big wedding, after all she had chosen to elope. But then she had Tommy, for her the biggest prize of all.

Never a dull moment in their relationship.

Handsome, good natured Catholic Tommy who would do anything to keep the peace. So the big day arrived and all the ladies took their seats in the synagogue. This time downstairs because of the wedding as the bride and groom made the vows under the canopy and the men stood together opposite them. Rose and Beryl were once again perched beside one another soaking up the occasion. Always having something to say, Rose whispered under breath that the Rabbi sounded like he was singing 'The Flight of the BumbleBee'.

Beryl had only gathered her composure when the next whisper exclaimed "Look at uncle Tommy, he's turned the wrong way and oh look now he's turned back too late and he's looking the wrong way again!"

RAE'S STORY

Nearly 80 years later Gladys and Percy Silverstein's son Mervyn and his darling wife Rae who live in Australia would come to visit N. Ireland, one stop on their world tour researching family history.

In the years after their marriages these granddaughters and cousins Gladys, her sister Jacqueline and Gloria would all emigrate to Australia.

As I opened the door of my studio at 52 to greet them the importance of our family connections smiled on us. The most special moment which brought tears to our eyes was, "Mervyn I have a present for you, this belonged to your grandfather." As I reached him a clothes hanger engraved with his grandfather's family name, given to me by a client. Little did I realise their visit was to bring a time of history into our home which was unimaginable.

1939–45 THE REIGN OF DEVILS, POLAND

As WWII was declared by Germany it was under the command of Adolf Hitler.

The horrific Nazi occupation of Poland began and is categorised as one of the most brutal chapters of WWII. Hitler named Hans Frank, a 39-year-old lawyer as Governor-General.

His son Niklas Frank would come to write about his father. His writings would lay bare intimate and strong accusations in his quest for the truth.

The Nazi Regime established approximately 42,500 camps and ghettos between 1933 and 1945. Concentration camps would eventually lead to selective extermination camps. These numbers are chilling.

All well documented in history, disastrously all too late.

When the German onslaught began in Poland the Jewish population were unaware of the desolation that was coming. The escalation of mass murder reached severe heights of immorality. Families could not escape.

In the midst of this Armageddon, a young man, Wolf Stawski, aged 26 found himself isolated from his first wife and daughter as they were located in numerous work camps. Survival meant subservience; it was the only purpose of his day, surrounded by fellow inmates, illness, weakness or sickness meant instant death, his youth being his saving grace as he was useful as a worker. How would he survive?

In the final spring of 1945, he sinisterly came under the notice of two SS commandants who mockingly chose him to play out a game with them. They marched him to a piece of ground.

His orders to grow a bed of flowers, sneering with humour that once a flower should die then so would he. He tried to explain that he knew nothing about flowers so one of the commandants told him he would help him work out when the weather would change and he then joyously walked over his hands until he broke all of his fingers.

No other words were exchanged, just callous laughter, these commandants were deaf to the thunderous silent voice of some.

Luckily for Wolf his camp was liberated a few months later and he along with other survivors found themselves in a Displaced Persons Camp. He had escaped Bergen Belsen alive. His wife Raszka and daughter Estera sadly did not, they were murdered in the Holocaust.

As with every other Jew, he then began the search for any of his family. Roaming the streets daily, acknowledging someone every now and again resolutely just catching his breath. Then by chance a man from his neighbourhood stopped him remarking,

"You know your brother is still alive, he rents a room," as he pointed upwards to a building.

Wolf slowly ascended the stairs into a sparse workroom. He could hear the rumble of a sewing machine in full flight and as he entered the room saw the frail angular body of a man focused only on his work. Without even turning round this man gestured to shelves holding a few bales of cloth and suggested to him to pick a piece if he wanted a jacket or a coat. Wolf nodded to himself, his heart lightened, still staring at the back of his brother's head. Then as he moved over to him he quietly said, "Do you not know who I am? Do you not recognise your brother?"

For the rest of their lives these two brothers even as they moved forward with their own families met every week to spend time together.

They would however leave Poland.

Countries of new residence were discussed and Haim was the first to make the move. By this time Wolf had met and married a fellow Belsen survivor Zossia within a short time of the end of the war in October 1945, their hearts lifted by the birth of their son Alex by 1946. In the desire to erase the trauma of what they had lived through meant that they too wanted to get as far away from Europe as they could, Poland was history to them and so the Stawskis immigrated to Australia arriving by sea into Melbourne in 1949, there they would join Haim.

Once settled both brothers established their own tailoring businesses. Wolf and Zossia would then look for a change and open a delicatessen far away from their tormentors and with a family of their own begin to live a different life. Gladly offering the hand of friendship constantly within their means to fellow survivors who continued to arrive from war torn countries. They also choose to keep their experiences largely to themselves. That was except when hidden emotions surfaced completely out of their control.

During his recovery from an operation Wolf under medication became nearly insane with fear convinced the SS were coming for him, believing they were trying to electrocute him. It was only his son-in-law who finally calmed him, reassured him he was safe, holding him close in his arms as he lay with him on his hospital bed. Wolf once he recovered had no recollection of this moment which terrorised his daughter. He and his wife mastered the power to bury all such memories.

Shockingly there would be another flashback of the dark days.

As Zossia served in her delicatessen she abruptly stopped in her tracks, colour drained from her face and she became ashen grey. Was she having a heart attack? her daughter pleaded. Fixated, staring wide eyed out the shop window, a blond woman freely striding down the other side of the street was a former Jewish policewoman who had terrorised fellow Jews in the camp.

Wolf and Zossia Stawski are the parents of Rae Silverstein. They escaped death in the extermination camps, they may have talked to each other about what they saw but never to their children and if the subject was raised Wolf only ever passed the comment, "It was a matter of luck."

1969 THE TROUBLES NORTHERN IRELAND

An ever-present backdrop of violence of a different nature.

The familiar security of childish safety disappeared, young adults knew no other way of life.

Self-defence along with self-preservation was born along with the shadows.

1970 Larne Grammar School beckoned and all I can say is

"There I found myself, courtesy of the 11 Plus Exam and with my parents' full approval, the single Catholic in my school Form Year and I found my greatest champion in Master Robert Beattie. A flamboyant character and great art teacher.

Thank God for Mr Beattie, I was never an academic."

This was a proud day for Neska Rolston, if anyone wanted this, it was she. This was something else for her to drop into the conversation next time she was with her siblings. Within the year her three grandchildren were all now attending grammar school, the fourth to follow. Competition, competition!

Beryl realised the creativity of the Leopolds had not been lost. Good job! She was not a pushy mother, nothing was further from the truth.

After all it was she who decided that Gerry and her should buy their daughter a sewing machine when she left grammar school.

Only too conscious of her artiness, having encouraged school projects over the years involving the creation of stage sets and 3D objects, never mind oil paint and pastels. Carpets covered in polystyrene balls, ovens overrun with plaster as miniature furniture was baked in them and glue stuck to tables and seats. It was quite odd that at that stage there was no mention of sewing.

Then of course there was measurable creativity on the Rolston side too. Country people, full of musicians and artists.

Thinking back to holidays in Fermanagh. Beryl's father Tommy, easily picked up where he left off on his last visit. A family of four brothers and two sisters, good natured and inoffensive with charming accents.

George and James worked the land while Packie worked his entire life on the local railway line and the eldest brother Josie, a master of trades, finally became an architect and a self-taught photographer. At no part of any day did George fail to entertain those around him, an innocent jovial man, so naturally humorous, forever singing at home or on the hill on the days he was ploughing the fields. Something their neighbours loved to hear as the wind carried his voice to their backdoor. Happiness and devilment shone out of George. All the brothers watched over their two sisters, May as it happens was an accomplished tailoress who back in her day was employed by the ladies of grand houses, residing at their homes for two weeks at a time to make bespoke clothes for their families. In fact if truth be told, this tall willowy damsel of calm disposition and sweet good nature ended up virtually dressing half the countryside. She would have needed immense patience, her only means of pressing a garment being with two hot irons heated over a casing on the fire and if clothes were not hand-stitched they were tirelessly sewn on a treadle machine. Nevertheless, May always would have generously taken the time to make dresses for her two nieces.

Beryl would often recall with humour, Auntie May and herself hiding in a back room when she was trying to avoid a customer and how as her own mother would have shifted her tea towel from shoulder to shoulder, May would have whispered, "Would you look at my mother trying to tell a lie."

Even I remember trying that ruse, telling my father just to say on the phone that I was not in. He got so caught up in the conversation and in response to the caller, "Hold on a second" and then proceed to ask me "What time will you be home?!"

Then there was Sissy, a stickler for etiquette, well suited as the private housekeeper in the local Manor House. A job she relished and perfected. Nothing escaped her gaze.

The Rolstons were a close-knit family, so if it was May who began the love of tailored dresses, it was Sissy who had introduced her niece to the vintage skill of crochet and lace making, forever referring to exquisite Carrickmacross lace. The traditional Irish lace, our national treasure.

Beryl would often recall the ease at which her daughter learned this skill. She had a hunch, hence the introduction of the sewing machine.

And so life continued. The government, political, social and paramilitary response engulfed Ulster. The result descending into 25 years of murder, destruction and dissent.

By 1979, The Troubles had been raging for ten years; the Province descended into a hotbed of turmoil, danger and financial ruin for many.

Notably, the light at the end of the tunnel was education, a way forward for the limited few. Easily carried, not easily got.

1979 Oct Ulster University Belfast

A fresh 19-year-old, I distinctly remember kissing my mother and stepping onto the footpath.

As I began walking away from home, and believe me I was walking on air, I turned and broadly smiled with total happiness at my very anxious mother and excitedly called out with absolute self-belief despite harbouring so many insecurities, "I am going to be a fashion designer!"

An innocent voice, full of romance but with a sense of purpose, attempting to reassure my mother that she and dad had given me strength to succeed. Beryl in turn replied, "Good."

It was all she could muster. The recent tragedy of Gerry's health had shaken her up badly. It seemed so unfair, life became even more unpredictable to her at this time.

1980 THE THRILL OF PARIS

Ulster University N. Irish 1st Year student trip.

GC Diary

So quite unannounced first thing one Monday morning, a circular was passed through the design room. Without hardly time to read it, our senior lecturer appeared from her office and in her high society clipped English accent, Adrienne revealed that a portfolio trip to Paris was on the cards. Music to my ears. God I was beside myself, Paris!

"Please do not walk down the Lisburn Road, it's dangerous in Belfast" my mother's words rang in my head as I walked up Melrose Street from my schoolfriend's rented house where I had stayed the night before. Suitcase in hand I do remember a slight cast of wind shudder past my shoulders, it was 5.30 am. Suddenly I did not feel quite so brave. Walking everywhere was my norm but surveying the empty streets and avenues in the distance, as they joined the main Lisburn Road, I strangely became very afraid. What could I do? I needed to keep walking, only I did not want to. I could hardly put one foot in front of the other with agitation.

Still looking straight ahead, attempting to eliminate my surroundings as I approached Tates Avenue, out of nowhere a car slowed down to my pace and the passenger spoke to me, asking if I was ok.

Not looking, I answered, "I'm fine thank you" as I kept on walking. Refusing to take no for an answer, he asked me again and this time offered me a lift.

Hardly daring to speak as the car crawled beside me, trying to assert my confidence, I finally glanced sideways and realised it was a police car, obviously patrolling the streets. So, yes of course I was taking the lift.

Not for one foolish second had I considered the dangerous climate in Belfast at that time.

On this occasion it was during the reign of the Shankill Butchers, their murderous campaign not yet uncovered.

Sure I believed my guardian angel was looking after me. Just as they had done the day I had walked outside the Co-Op to cross over to the Art College, when I stopped sharply in my tracks as I looked down the barrel of a soldier's gun. Kneeling behind the pillars of the college in the distance he had me in his line of sight. If I was scared, so was he, as he quickly lowered his weapon and turned away. He knew I saw him that day on York Street.

So off we 1st year fashion students travelled to Paris with a full itinerary.

Pret-a-Porter Shows, Fashion Houses, Art Galleries & Museums.

French style and culture, the architecture, it was all awe-inspiring.

Forty years ago, two extremes of residency from Larne to Paris.

LATER THAT YEAR

Home now from Paris and ready to take the world on, a trip to Dublin turned up. As part of her university studies my sister Roisin was based there for a year and she was never short of visitors, myself included.

Time had moved so swiftly for the senior Leopold girls who were left and now two of them were living in the city.

Of course the family networking never ceased and news travelled fast.

The draw and expectation of family visits could never escape that Jewish tight noose. If the aunts knew you were in the area, you would need to turn up at some stage.

Roisin of course was well caught, she would faithfully visit Auntie Millie and Uncle Albert now in the 80s every Saturday. They just loved to hear all the latest.

So the rumour made it to their apartment, well, it was hardly a rumour, Rose, their daughter would have telephoned them to let them know, because Beryl her cousin would have telephoned Rose to let her know.

Then we were told that we were expected.

Forget about work or nightlife, first on the agenda was what time suited for the family visit. Decision made mid to late afternoon Roisin and I loaded up with flowers and chocolates began the 40-minute walk from her student house in Rathgar to the South Circular Road into Rathmines.

This particular weekend trip which I vividly recall would throw up an introduction and a challenge.

For Auntie Millie and Uncle Albert would have unexpected guests waiting to meet us.

We did wonder that she was a little bit fussed and flurried when she opened the door to greet us and welcome us in.

Glancing up the hall we could already see her dining table as always perfectly set, the best china on display and tasty sandwiches and cakes for the taking.

"Take your coats off, take your coats off," she gestured as if to make sure we were going to stay for a while and of course we did as we were told. Like lightning she had them hung up before we even got into the room, hardly having had time to say hello. What was up? We thought.

Then it all became clear. Roisin and I were to be introduced to Auntie Lallie and Uncle Eric, very much in their seniority now.

Lallie is our grandmother Neska's younger sister.

This was indeed such a surprise and as it turned out, great fortune.

LALLIE LEOPOLD

1917 Rose and Philip would have their last child, a daughter named Lallie. So petite, blonde and vivacious. Just like the rest of them she commanded attention, processive of a tremendous personality, sharp and smart to say the least, as her niece Beryl recollects and the memory of a child is vivid. A witty off-the-wall entertainer, forever seeing humour, incapable of not voicing her opinion.

Applauded for her beautiful figure, Lallie was compelled to wear the latest fashion as she would enjoy the chase of competition for the best dressed. Never to be described as a shrinking violet, with her overly confident, colourful, direct opinions, demands and sparkling attitude.

She should surely have been on a film set.

On one particular occasion as Beryl happened to be on her way up to visit her grandfather after work she saw this vision walking down Kingsmere Avenue in front of her. She could see this damsel was walking very slowly, placing her feet so perfectly. Beryl was even more impressed when they caught up with each other as it dawned on her that this sublime figure was Auntie Lallie. she exclaimed! "What a beautiful suit Auntie Lallie, it is so elegant on you, I love it."

Incapable of taking her mind off her balance, Lallie breathing fire strode on, maintaining her posture, declaring under her breath, "These bliddy shoes are killing me, I can't walk in them. I need to get them off!"

What made it worse for her of course was that the avenue sloped downhill. Eventually as they reached the safety of the house, Beryl recalls the shoes hurtling past her narrowly missing her head and smacking into the front door.

Lallie would marry her husband Eric Davies and eventually leave Belfast to live in Dublin where they were immersed in the rag trade scene, a different arena from Belfast. They too had a son whom they adored, called after the bombing of Belfast during WWII, Selwyn Blitz Davies.

The distance gave them their own freedom.

BACK TO AUNTIE MILLIE'S SITTING ROOM IN DUBLIN

Of course the topic of fashion was brought up and Millie could hardly contain herself announcing with such pleasure that I was now studying fashion design and that it could only come from their father. Waxing lyrical for this chosen path as I sunk further and further back into my chair, sensing just a tad of competition between them. I had no notion of how deep the feelings were about tailoring skills, nor did I know that their son was also in the trade. At that stage I was only full of the romance of Paris. However!

"I defy anyone to put a sleeve in like my Selwyn!" Auntie Lallie declared crushing me slightly.

Funny, that was the first time I ever felt the chill of direct scepticism.

They did not stay long as it happens they had already been there for some time, Auntie Millie did attempt to soften the blow by lamenting "Why can she never take her coat off? "

My thoughts were, I will prove myself to Auntie Lallie, unaware that she had raised my self-ambition with her singular statement and certainly no idea how closely I was listening to her.

Sadly we would never meet again.

THE BEGINNING OF BIG DREAMS
PART ONE

1984 Larne Home Town

"Please get up, would you not go for it? It would give you security, what have you to lose?"

Head under my pillow I tried to drown out the pleading words of my mother.

A job had presented itself in the Fashion Department of Ulster University.

At that point, I did not want to teach, I had done it for three months and I knew it was not for me. I suppose it was an uneasiness of the lack of opportunities back in 1984 that made me finally get dressed and head for the train to Belfast.

The interview panel of Artists and University Directors made the decision for me.

"We think you should take your art further. See where it takes you."

Words and advice I anxiously wanted to hear, not remotely comprehending the bars I would come to set myself.

1985 January GERALDINE CONNON established.

Youth has no fear of the unknown.

Pointless listening to doubters, I kept my secret weapon to myself. My heritage. A fashion designer in 1984 in a country town! It was ludicrous.

"Well now I'm sorry we don't get jobs like that around here," emphasised the unemployment officer, I'm sure, flashing a pathetic glance my way.

There was however, another little problem, in that ridiculously, opening official letters, reading receipts or looking at bank statements never took priority. But then, as time would tell.

This emerging Love Affair was not about paperwork.

It was about art and it was about fashion and in my time it was on the cusp of "designer fever", fed by the emerging world romance surrounding Princess Diana and her style. The passion she displayed towards the underdog, the unknowns, struck a chord, that appeal hit all possibilities. A commission from the Palace perhaps. That would work.

1986 BELFAST, LOWER DONEGALL STREET

A rare day out in the city after lunch and a jaunt around the shops with a couple of friends who shall remain nameless, we found ourselves with a bit of time to kill. As we walked towards the Art College our attention was drawn to this appealing sign on the side of a doorway.

How could we resist?

"Let's go, let's go. it's just fun," words which echoed for years.

"Okay, let's go."

"Hold out your hand my dear..." Looking clearly and directly into her eyes, Maisie, a renowned Belfast spiritualist exclaimed, "I don't know what it is you are looking for my dear but it is not on this earth!"

AND THE WALL GOT HIGHER

C'EST LA VIE
1954 12TH APRIL KINGSMERE AVENUE

When the morning dawned over Cavehill it was just like any other fresh spring day.

North Belfast folk were immersed in their usual daily routines. A new generation had moved in. Life was certainly changing in the workplace, commerce was shifting and industry was developing in many different directions, certainly away from clothing manufacture anyhow.

Economically it was difficult to compete with foreign manufacture. The Leopolds by now no longer needed to concern themselves, the decision had been taken in 1952 to close up shop.

Philip had already retired from the business a number of years previously, he had lived his life in a moment of time where bespoke tailoring reigned and industrial manufacture exploded in the UK and Ireland. That had all passed and youth was not on his side now to take up a new mantle of business competition.

Nevertheless he still drew people to him, always plenty of visitors. If it wasn't family, it was friends and even when he first retired it was some of the girls from his factory begging him to come back.

"Please Boss, please come back. We will carry you up the stairs."

So he had all the time in the world to reflect and reminisce.

Everyone had grown up around him and a very special few of them had passed way too soon. Yet no one was prepared for how this day would unfold and the cast of fate because suddenly a cold breeze dimmed the light.

With no grand fanfare for his immense achievements, his most precious thoughts kept to himself, a proud man, a generous giver who wholeheartedly loved his family, a noble fighter who made his mark in his adopted home of Belfast was taken from the stage.

It was Bea who found him propped up in bed, sleeping, she thought.

Philip Lepar Leopold finally let go of his life. That great chat became silent along with his legacy. He would have understood that it is either in your blood or not. It was in his and it is in mine.

Hearts were stricken. Emotions were out of control. The daughters wailed and sobbed for their father as they gathered round his humble wooden coffin Beryl whispered to her mother to calm down, "Granda wouldn't like it."

When the Rabbi took charge and the prayers commenced a certain solemnity took over. Heads were bowed low as the family moved with respect to lay their father to rest. As with tradition then, only a son can say the Kaddish (memorial prayer), three times a day for 11 months until Matzevah (tombstone) is consecrated. The belief is that the reciting of Kaddish helps the soul to rest in peace.

Sonny would come to say these prayers for his father, prayers which he had been charged with almost 20 years earlier when he recited them for his mother, Rose.

Now one last gesture of everlasting love would remind them all of their father's soul.

As the family made that final journey to Carnmoney Cemetery from Cavehill, quite some distance away they could already see where their father's final resting place was to be.

It was the only one in the graveyard.

Philip being the man he was, had made sure of that, for when his beloved Rose was buried, he, against all Jewish tradition of no flowers, had planted a tree on her grave. No ordinary tree, a cypress tree that would grow strong and tall and wrap its roots around her, like his arms.

Had he not vowed to protect her and them all those years ago, a young immigrant couple full of hopes, desires and big plans.

They did know everlasting love.

Fear not nor grieve at my departure, you whom I have loved so much, for my roots and yours are forever entwined.

He had known from his place on Cavehill that he could always see where he had laid her to rest and now he was to be beside her at last.

That Russian love affair was a 'fait accompli'.

Beryl stood quietly in the background, holding tight to her grief.

"My God, Granda is gone."

Strangely today as I have come to this chapter I am resigned to recount, that of his death, he comes alive again.

On this very day, 17th January 2020 his portrait is circulating North

Belfast thanks to John McVicker and the *Shankill Mirror* which the readership swells to at least 10,000 people. I want that for him.

This was a public search for information, any information on men or women of the Leopold workforce. Beryl wistfully says, "He would be so proud."

1956 LARNE: THE ROLSTON HOUSEHOLD

So the time had finally come. Tommy and Neska had a wedding to celebrate. Emotions were high, Tommy knew her grandfather's passing two years earlier had left Beryl bereft so no words were spoken about him in the run up to the day because again the Belfast family were not expected.

Gerry had met her grandfather, she took solace in knowing they knew each other. It was to be a quiet affair. No fuss.

Ceremony 8.30 am and a wedding breakfast in the Kings Arms in her home town Larne. This shy young lady took comfort in her father's mellow way as he took her hand in his and linked it through his arm. Stepping on to the path of their terrace on the Bank Road the two of them started the first of their walks of the day down to the waiting wedding car. Unbeknown to her in his excitement he had told all the neighbours to watch out for her and there they were lined up all only too happy to join in. That was the closest Tommy Rolston ever came to showing pride.

Ceremony over everyone was in high spirits as they made their way over to the reception. Beryl's wedding day was about to be complete.

As she and Gerry greeted their guests, who would suddenly appear at the door? Auntie Bea. Beautiful Auntie Bea unaccompanied but dressed to the nines. After the losses she and Sam bore, Bea would slowly claim herself back. Still possessive of innocent childishness in her manner believing as the first born her siblings should pay heed to her. What's more, with her fathers' passing she now was matriarch of the family.

Knowing the Leopold love of weddings, it would have been the only conversation in Belfast.

The final decision played out after much debate.

Bea chose to do what she knew Beryl's grandfather would have done. She was braver now. I can just imagine her talking to herself, letting those around her make their own choices.

This was a wedding, an occasion to celebrate not to be missed. The surprise was hers to claim.

1969 BELFAST ROYAL VICTORIA HOSPITAL

Beryl and her Uncle Sonny stood outside the hospital entrance. It was a chilly night 8th October as Beryl pulled the collar of her coat up around her neck to try and keep warm. Life was so different now that she was a mother to four children and her husband was beginning to struggle with his health. Unrest was creeping into the city, not yet having reached the outlying towns and suburbs.

Still there were other pressing worries.

Auntie Bea was unwell, she was frightened, lonely and seemed so vulnerable and weak in her bed. Beryl was frightened too. Feeling helpless as she tried to reassure her that the doctors had everything under control.

Sonny for his part attempted to lighten the mood telling her she was worrying for no reason. They stayed with her for the full visiting time and when they came to say goodbye Beryl and she hugged each other so close. Bea held her niece's hand barely able to let go, as Beryl kissed her and they bid each other Godspeed.

Outside Sonny hailed a taxi and they climbed in.

Within a couple of minutes Sonny suddenly recognised the driver was Rinty Monaghan, the champion boxer and the conversation began.

Of course he applauded him for his successes and told him how his father and they had been to all his matches. Rinty had freely said how life had changed for him since his hay day but they could see he was a jolly kind character with no malice or regrets in his heart.

Beryl just quietly listened to the two men talking but she had her own memories of Rinty. Namely the time when she helped him and his brothers in their excitement to choose a fur coat for their mother as a treat when she worked in Barnett Huttons many moons ago and Rinty was on top of the world.

Auntie Bea died later that night.

As it turns out, she was not on her own at the end after all.

Sonny's eldest son Leslie, who was named for her own son whom she lost at Christmas 1941 was studying medicine at Queen's University and was a junior houseman in the Royal.

An emergency call came into the doctor's station where Leslie just happened to be and he joined the consultant on the alarm.

Leslie was with her, that would at least give Beryl solace.

Poor Auntie Bea had peace at last, she who had suffered so much and had been so brave could never really hide her pain. The thing about her was at least she tried very hard to do so.

Twelve years later handsome Tommy Rolston would die.

Try as everyone did, no one could fill the void.

Neska would struggle desperately to live without him, yet to no avail.

She died three lonely years later, by this time a tiny bird still feisty, in a little world of her own.

It was only a short precious time from when the two darlings so very frail now, would have stood in the doorway of their home on the Bank Road terrace to wave to my Irish dancing friend and travelling companion Leslie and I as we passed by on the train from Belfast and the Art College at the end of the day. We could surely see the sweethearts and we made sure they could see us because Leslie would wave his white silk scarf out of the window of the door whilst the two of us braced ourselves to balance in the corridor as the old carriages shunted towards to the town center. Such is love.

THE BEGINNING OF BIG DREAMS
PART TWO

1983 RECORDING CONTRACTS in TOWN

With a vision of his own, a new entrepreneur on the block Charlie Tosh launched Hawk Records. Deciding to join the competitive music world, he had set his sights on Rinty Monaghan for his record label.

The song, 'When Irish Eyes are Smiling'. Which the champion boxer sang after every victory in the ring. All magnificent 52 of them.

Rinty now in his later life worked in a garage these days, yet he was more than popular on the cabaret scene all over the North of Ireland.

Would Rinty be a success on vinyl? "Of course he will, he is a legend," says Charlie stoutly.

The next artist in Mr Tosh's sights was Vincent Rolston and his band Gemini Three, singing 'Remember Me' composed by Vincent.

Seems Rinty was going to dip in and out of the Rolston family one way or another. Vincent was Beryl's cousin from Carnboy in Fermanagh.

He would go on to success with his group while Rinty's new dream of the music arena at this time would hardly get off the ground when he died in March the following year. Vincent attended his poignant funeral and memorial service in St. Patrick's Chapel, Donegal Street. By this time the adjacent Leopold workshop stood vacant and silent, no rumble of machines now.

The cabaret circuit would keep his spirit alive for a few more years.

Yet this era of entertainment which began in the 1950s never really recovered from the massacre of The Miami Showband in 1975, and would die out by the mid-1980s.

Not even entertainers could escape the brutality of 'The Troubles'.

SMITHFIELD BELFAST

1986 June

My mission. Straight to Belfast, park at Smithfield, which at that time was only more of a market area with a makeshift car park, run in and buy the present and get home. There were still security barriers to negotiate in the city but the British Army had finally vacated the former beautiful Grand Central Hotel a couple of years earlier which they had used as military headquarters. So although there was still a mighty police presence at least army Saracens were not driving alongside pedestrians in the middle of the City.

There was great excitement amongst all of us. Friends from university had just had their first child and everyone wanted to celebrate.

We shared a car between us in our house, a red ford escort with a black cloth roof which was my older brother Brian's pride and joy.

Happy with my purchase I walked back to the car.

What car? Standing dazed in the middle of Smithfield it was nowhere to be seen.

Then the jittery little man in the ticket hut says

"Ah love, your car's just been stolen. You may take yourself round to Glenravel Street Police Station. You can report it there! I just lifted the barrier because they would have broken my barrier and wrecked your windscreen."

Just like that. I was a bit dazed yet as I made my way over to the station I felt a glimmer of happiness thinking how opportunistic it was to get inside the building which had been granda's former workplace and incidentally as it so happened looked as if it was still the original booking office of dark wooden imposing high walls and bench for me to perch on.

Two hours later I'm then sitting in the back of a police Land Rover on route to retrieve my car which the very kind sergeant in charge, told me had been stopped only minutes after it had been stolen. Undercover officers surveying the area had watched the boys steal it and following a short chase they efficiently apprehended them.

Then with no warning, a call came through and minutes from getting my car I was trailblazing into West Belfast to join an army convoy under attack from stone throwing youths. Fast forward another two hours and back at the Grosvenor Road roundabout, just on the cusp of trouble with land rovers parked on every hard shoulder the order was given to get out.

Soldiers scurried to vantage points, hunched down on their knees, guns at the ready and the driver said,

"Now Miss you just go over to your car, get in and drive off home."

Eyes staring like a rabbits in headlights, shaking with fear I walked to my car, abandoned and crashed up onto the central reservation of the roundabout, two inches from the barriers, got in, lifted the car thief's jacket for no particular reason and then set it back down, reversed onto the road and drove myself home to Larne. Eyes wide shut.

C'EST LA VIE N. IRELAND

GC DIARY

OCTOBER 1996, WHITLA HALL, QUEEN'S UNIVERSITY BELFAST

As the City comes to the end of the working day it descends into chaos, consequently brought to a stand-still with well-placed bomb scares.

Weaving in and out of the car lanes over low pavements around the Albert Clock. No time to spare!

The reception at the Whitla Hall Queen's University was already underway. This was the Guinness Fashion Awards, The main fashion event on the calendar every year.

Undeterred by any danger, totally dismissive of the atmosphere of fear, I crossed from the North to the South of the City negotiating traffic at a standstill finally reaching my destination and slipping hardly noticed into the back of the reception room where the speeches and presentations are coming to a close. As it turns out, leaving rehearsals late afternoon to briefly travel home for a short break had not been such a clever idea after all, once the IRA had launched their prepared attack to shut the city down.

Anyhow the Show still went on as life did regardless in Ulster. For the third time the top Designer of the Year Award that evening came my way, the fourth the following year.

As the headlines of the *Belfast Telegraph* read the next day the dual sets of lives being lived out filled the copy.

2nd November 1996 Reference: BELFAST TELEGRAPH 127th Year

Front Page, GERALDINE WINS AGAIN IN TRUE FASHION – IRA DENY SUMMIT IN MAYO

Celebs toast the cream of Ulster's Designers

The Guinness Fashion Award was sadly a bittersweet moment as I could hardly rise from the seat to receive it having finally lost my precious father earlier in the year.

As the PR team frantically searched for the winner along the upper gallery it was out of their control, there I sat on my hands downstairs amongst family and friends, my inner circle.

Before the winner was to be announced my mind and senses were raised. Knowing that the models backstage would soon hit the catwalk.

"I think the girls are putting the wigs on! Have I won this? No that's not possible but wait I am sure they are putting the wigs on! Oh stop with this, just get on with it. Who is the winner?" Let's get this over with and I can forget about this madness."

This had been an earlier thought in my mind as I had made my way through the city. Telling myself that yes, it would be a useful Trophy to have. The win would add to the other three and would be good for business. On the other hand not to win would just allow me to slip back into a normal life and remove the agony of expectations. For the longest ten seconds as the crowd raised the roof with deafening applause, head down I gathered my composure.

The *Belfast Telegraph* front page had reached more households than one can imagine and Beryl took a call out of the blue.

Reaching the phone to me after a very happy conversation she said,

"That's your Auntie Phyllis on the phone, she wants to congratulate you on last night's win."

"Well done my dear, I just said to Sonny, we have missed out so much on Beryl's children, well done, we are very proud of you. You know this is in your genes."

18TH APRIL 1997 FASHION SPECTACULAR, BELFAST CITY HALL

A charity close to my heart, Shopmobility.

This show I was looking forward to, never mind the catwalk performance. There was a chance of viewing the back rooms and corridors of the City Hall which I knew only too well was the extra draw as for the first time ever my Uncle Danny was attending. An invitation he had surprisingly accepted with a grin and nod as he peered over his newspaper at me. I had pondered momentarily whether he was mellowing a bit now that he had retired. Dare I believe it. You see, dad never made it to any of my shows although he was never away from my studio. How he would have enjoyed them, no one more aware of the value of competition. Of this I am very sure thinking back to my sister Roisin and our Irish dancing days. The greatest hobby of many generations including ours when dad joyfully escorted us round half of Ireland.

So then with the pressure on for the latest performance I stood sewing at the machines not even time to sit, when I took the call.

Danny is in Intensive Care at Antrim Hospital, he has suffered a heart attack.

We had sat together through the night until morning not realising this would be our last tête-à-tête. "Get into your work," he said, to which I replied, "Yes, shortly." Shockingly as he was not a demonstrative man Danny then covered his hand over my hand clenching it tightly as he pulled the oxygen mask off with the other shaking his head in despair knowing his time was limited.

"I tried to reassure him everything would be fine and he just needed to rest." I cried to relatives later that day in desolation.

Even though I had made it into work by 9.30 am frantically still standing sewing at my machines, not for one second did I expect my brother to call. I remember glancing over my shoulder and seeing his reflection in the mirror on the hall stand. Frazzled, my thoughts were equally agitated. I've no time to talk.

Leaning against the doorframe for support for sure Brian's words killed me. "Geraldine, Uncle Danny is dead."

Everything went black, unbearable. Uncle Danny's death solidified my father's. Now he was gone too, a complex emotionally broken genius. So much so that cold medical documents revealing the cause of death noted that Danny's heart burst.

That very evening the City Hall Fashion Extravaganza still had to be presented, my request being that my uncle's name was not to be mentioned." Do not show me kindness" I had to work.

10 APRIL 1998 THE GOOD FRIDAY AGREEMENT was signed effective from 2nd DECEMBER 1999 (Beryl's 67th birthday).

As I sat in the Green Room at UTV Studios Belfast waiting for the evening's live *Gerry Kelly Talk Show* having been brought in as an assistant to David Emmanuel, ex-husband and partner of Elizabeth Emmanuel, designers of Princess Diana's wedding dress, on a special weight loss feature they were running, the atmosphere suddenly changed. The other side of life thundered.

Senior politicians both North and South of Ireland alongside Tony Blair, British Prime Minister signed the Belfast Agreement, a document which ended most of the violence of the Troubles and served as a major development in the peace process.

Welcomed by many weary of the conflict and murder, it earned two senior N. Ireland politicians the joint Nobel Peace Prize, David Trimble and John Hume. Yet unleashed explosive anger amongst others and the leader of the main opposing political party stormed through the Green Room as I sat there not daring to breathe, into the adjacent makeup room shadowed by his redheaded security guard.

As I stared at them, they stared at me, Northern Irish people with completely opposite passions, visions and focus, I knew it was history in the making.

TWO DAYS LATER
12TH APRIL 1998 BBC, MAKING A DIFFERENCE SHOW

Grand Opera House Belfast

The powers that be in the arts and media launched a series of one off shows in celebration of well deserving individuals who had suffered through the Troubles in many walks of life. The directors and producers' vision to show a side of N. Ireland that had survived mainly in the background for years, possibly showing a way forward in the entertainment and new social scene which the Province was slowly embarking on.

Highly accomplished artists worldwide were invited to perform at a star studded evening at the Grand Opera House Belfast. These included singers, comedians, musicians and actors,

Ant and Dec, Pete Postlethwaite, Olivia Newton John, Patrick Kielty, Cliff Richard, Brian Kennedy, Amanda Burton, Nana Mouskouri and the list goes on. In this atmosphere of variety, my name was brought into the arena and I was invited to meet with the producer at the BBC. That meeting went well and my contract was signed.

A catwalk performance with live music, not much to ask.

I remember being very sure of the musicians I wanted to play for me. That worked well when I put my request to him as these guys were booked already. 'Different Drums', they were my choice, special guests only the previous week on a Gala Show celebrating Phil Coulter's life, televised from the Waterfront Hall. That is when I first saw them perform.

By the end of this week I was to witness history again, unrecorded history.

9th JANUARY 1998 Dr Mo Mowlam took an unprecedented political gamble and met with senior UDA prisoners in the Maze prison. The outcome led to the loyalist inmates giving their political representatives the go-ahead to remain in talks in the Stormont process which were to resume that following Monday.

Mowlam met five senior UDA inmates for 50 minutes and afterwards held less formal separate meetings with IRA and UVF prisoners, each lasting around 15 minutes.

Her first comments to the press conference were to apologise to those victims of the Troubles who contacted her to complain about her decision to meet the prisoners and also to thank those relatives of victims who had offered their support.

She declared that she had a duty to the people of N. Ireland to use all means in her power to ensure the peace process was taken further.

In her words, "Talks are the only way forward."

The Taoiseach, Mr Ahern paid tribute to Dr Mowlam saying she was "brave" to take the initiatives she had taken.

"It's good to see that Mo Mowlam's efforts are getting somewhere."

This was the official media report the following day on the sequence of events. What did not make the news copy happened at a WAVE concert the previous evening at Queen's University. WAVE is a cross community, voluntary, regional organisation to offer care and support to anyone bereaved, injured or traumatised through the Troubles.

Through my network of close friends I learned that Different Drums were to be playing at this concert and it seemed to be the perfect opportunity to introduce myself. Having taken a seat early I listened thoughtfully to the testimonies of victims and applauded the entertainers. It was an evening charged with high emotions. Then without warning the lights went up and initially a sense of fear threatened to disrupt the hall.

This was N. Ireland, anything could happen. There was a commotion of sorts at the entrance doors as a huddled group of people started to move slowly up the side of the room. Those on the aisle seats caught the first glance as astonished voices filtered through the rows.

A measured cheering broke out and then the clapping started. A ripple of excitement caught the crowd as we realised that this unexpected speaker was Dr Mo Mowlam and her security. Before the group reached the stage the applause was staggering, Everyone present rose to their feet caught up in the significance of the moment.

Sir Kenneth Bloomfield at that time N. Ireland Victims Commissioner eventually found his moment to announce the surprise visit and introduce the lady herself. Understanding the emotions and sacrifices that this audience had experienced during the conflict Mo Mowlam had the foresight and vision to repeat in person her actions from earlier in the day to reassure all victims the importance of dialect and that she as a politician would be doing everything in her power to bring reconciliation.

Her words clearly said that she was in no way undermining the work that WAVE contributed to the wider community. The charity and all of its volunteers had her highest respect and support.

The applause roared loudly again. I nearly forgot why I was there in the first place as I shook hands with Stephen Matier of Different Drums when the curtain fell.

DUALITY OF LIFE CONTINUES

March 2000 *SUNDAY LIFE* newspaper Charity Fashion Show
WATERFRONT HALL
Another show, another venue and still loyal followers of fashion flocked to claim the best seats.

19th March 2000 Front Page Editorial
SUNDAY LIFE UK Newspaper of the Year Reference; The copy displayed two passionate opposing images.

KING RAT TAPE SHOCK Wright accuses MI5 from beyond the grave.
FASHION SHOW Picture Special. Catwalk image from GC Collection.

As if predicted that same evening Neska Leopold Rolston's sister Millie (Minka) Coss died, aged 93.

1995–2000 A sad toll rolled out for the Connon family. Twelve people both family and friends in our chat group, all died. The world as I knew it was disintegrating around me. What brought this cast of fate down? It was not a war crime this time. As I clung to my father's whisper to me on his deathbed as I moved his pillows to comfort him, in the midst of our despair knowing we were running out of time, he still showed his strength.

"Do you need any money Geraldine?"

"No dad, thankyou."

"GET BEHIND THE WALL"

"Feb 2000 GC STUDIO LARNE

THE POWER OF SPIRIT

A lonesome figure standing in the hallway gazed with a fixed stare through the glass of the front door.

It had been four years of working in emotional isolation. Bereavement is a lonely place. Breaking the silence, the phone rings.

"Hello, I'm looking for the Connons, would I have the right number?"

A thick Ballymena accent echoed.

"Yes, this is the Connons. Are you looking for Danny?"

A resigned voice enquired as that was the norm.

"No, actually I'm looking for Gerry. He's been on my mind for so long and I thought I would give it one last go to find him, I'm not in the best of health."

"Yes you have found us. Gerry was my father."

"Well I need to tell you, he has been on my mind for some time and I thought I would give it one last go to find him.

"I have been compelled to find him, Gerry saved my life, he was my greatest friend. I have so much to tell you about him.

Was he still a sharp dressed man? That's how I remember him."

This call came on 29th Feb 2000 the first leap year anniversary of Gerry Connon's death.

There are those who would not see any significance to this and there are those who would take solace in it. My spirit resurfaced.

As I turned and looked up to the sky through the window of the door, I knew it was him.

GERRY

"Are you sleeping dad" we often asked
" No I'm resting my eyes" he would say
"Does he like that new album", proud of my choices
When I hear, a blank tape would have been better any day.
Who ever knew there were films about love?
Our TV only featured the 'Wild West'
"What would you do? what do you think?"
"Sure love all you can do is your best"

– *Geraldine Connon*

2000 BELFAST: ROSE COSS
DAUGHTER OF MILLIE AND ALBERT COSS

"Here is your invitation, now who all are coming? Just give me your list."

Rose excitedly presented cousin Beryl the Invitation to Dublin.

"Daddy and Mammy will want everyone there."

Albert, having just celebrated his 99th birthday, had moved to Dublin in the 1950s after Philip had died. He and his wife Millie Leopold, 91 now had happily lived the second part of their lives in Southern Ireland.

And so it was to be. The extended Leopold Family gathered in Dublin.

Coming from as near as Belfast and as far as Jerusalem, Israel and the USA.

15th March 2000 DUBLIN JEWISH HOME

Monsieur Henri de Coignac, the French Ambassador to Ireland presented Albert Coss the white enamel cross of 'The Legion d'Honneur' in recognition of his courageous service during WWI.

"This distinction pays homage to all those both French and foreigners who fought on French soil to defend the cause of liberty.

It is a symbol of the gratitude of the French people towards those who risked their lives in order to defend our borders and to enable human rights to prevail. Albert Coss is one of these men."

Pride resonated around the home, it was truly a joyous event. Familiar faces enjoying catching up and new faces keen to speak.

Step up the enigmatic Eric Silver, journalist, war office correspondent, author and nephew of Albert.

"Let me give you my card. You will come and visit us next time you are in Israel," He graciously nodded to me.

"Mmmm now I would have no reason to go to Israel, can't see that happening." The startled look on Eric's face, questioning my response, quickly led me to add, "Well, actually maybe next time Brian, my brother is working in Jerusalem I'll come and stay with him and we will come to visit you." Eric smiled with approval.

TWO MONTHS LATER:
JERUSALEM ISRAEL: TOMB OF KING DAVID

GC Diary

Slipping discreetly past security guards as if in slow motion David quietly walked ahead. The spiritual atmosphere engulfed us as we made our way through the ancient doorways touching each mezuzah as we entered a new room. Then just suddenly without warning he startled me as I was so wrapped up in my surroundings and turning around he announced "We are here."

I looked closely into his face, unable to speak, realising that with just two steps forward, I was standing in front of the Tomb of King David.

Do you know how deep my love is for you
You have claimed your piece of my heart
As long as the day and night plays out
Never ever will we be apart. GC

As we walked back out into the sunlight, I turned to David and asked him if he had said a prayer for his father, he replied yes he had, with a heavy heart because his loss had been quite recent.

"I will never forget that face of sadness."

David was the driver and guide I hired to show me a whirlwind of sights while I was in Israel for four days. Two days working on the Eurovision Competition, two days free time.

Israel as a destination had never been even a passing thought in my mind; strangely once I stepped onto land, the surroundings felt familiar, the atmosphere beguiling and my plan was to seize the moment.

Taking in the spectacle of Mount Zion parked in David's taxi, the entire place was mesmerising, thronging with visiting pilgrims, locals, holy men, onlookers. I thoughtfully chose my words and carefully wrote my prayer. Was this really happening?

Within minutes I was reverently yet nervously walking towards the Western Wailing Wall.

My heart was racing. I looked back and David nodded reassuringly, not at all offended that I had asked him to get out of his taxi while I wrote my intentions in peace.

I slotted my script into the Wall, stepped back a few paces and held my station edgily waiting for an official to put their hand on my shoulder and question my permission to even be there.

(that onerous hand again!)

I was in a good place.

Finally what seemed too soon, I slowly walked back outside the boundary. That was it.

Jerusalem 91000…

"Eric, it's Geraldine, we met at Uncle Albert's Medal presentation in Dublin.

Something very strange has happened! I'm going to be dressing the singers for Ireland at this year's Eurovision Song Contest in Israel, it's hard to believe."

"I know all about it!" Eric exclaimed, "Rose wrote to tell me, I received her letter this morning!"

So as it happened Rose's cousin Eric Silver born in Leeds in 1935 was a highly acclaimed war correspondent and author of three titles.

The Book of the Just (1992), *Begin: The Haunted Prophet* (1984), *Begin: A Biography* (1984): described by one of his closest friends as "an old fashioned journalist, in the best sense of the word." In 1960 he was employed by the *Guardian* newspaper moving up from copy editor to reporter. That was the start of his career writing for the *Guardian* and the *Observer*. He, as he put it, reporting on war and peace. In 1975 he was chosen as chairman of the Israel Foreign Press Association followed by four years in the 1980s in India. By the end of his time there he decided he wanted to settle in Jerusalem and that is exactly what he did along with his family. Eric chose Israel.

I hurriedly freshened up, not much time as I had just barely returned from the Old City with David. "Oh I am so looking forward to seeing Eric," I said to myself. Remembering fondly our introduction in Dublin, his calmness and kindness.

As I came out of the lift turning into the reception he simultaneously walked in through the hotel entrance doors. We embraced each other with wide smiles for the newly found family. Dinner in Jerusalem was totally unexpected, an evening which never in my imagination would I have thought to find myself in.

"So are you enjoying your trip?" Eric asked

"Amazing. I enjoyed the experience of the Eurovision, backstage was utter organised chaos at every turn lots of highly competitive and passionate performers.

I do love competition, it's the spice of life. Today I found myself a great taxi driver and apart from everywhere we got to visit, tomorrow he is taking me to Masada and the Dead Sea. I hope I float."

As is my thing, I had taken myself for a walk that morning and after an hour sat down at the side of the road to eat some lunch. Just taking in my surroundings suddenly over the brow of the hill came a marching regiment of about 80 soldiers. So it was at that point my N. Irish common sense told me to shift myself back in the direction I had just come from and then, must have been heaven sent, David pulled his taxi over. "So where do you want to go?". Once I enlightened him to my now Jewish crusade and quest for seeing as much as possible of the region, he was onboard. All in response to his question, "So what is a blonde doing in Jerusalem?"

"Tomorrow we head for Masada,"

"Masada. That's a long journey! Are you sure he's Jewish?"

My hosts exclaimed, slightly startled!! "Oh he's definitely Jewish, he is called David." Looking back, that could have been deemed a little bit suspicious considering he had introduced me to a guide earlier in the day who showed me around Bethlehem and who just happened to be called Joseph!

Sometimes even I am dazed at my own naivety.

"Today my taxi driver took me to the Tomb of King David. I had a sense of peace, having been able to pray for my grandmother in that she was at peace with her father and he with her.

David knew the relevance and significance of that for me while I am in Israel after all. It was the first and only thought which came to my mind when I walked into the crypt. I could hardly believe I was there.

It brought me so much satisfaction. I was happy to do that for them."

Mixed marriage, the crime of culture whatever your race, religion or nationality, not for the lovers for the aggrieved onlooking loved ones.

As it happens Eric and Brigid's daughter Rachel was visiting from London and joined us for dinner. She had inherited her father's gift for writing having numerous titles under her own belt so plenty of chat was had and the debate of mixed marriage continued with a new subject.

I was intrigued.

This time it was a colleague of Eric's on the BBC World Service, Indian royalty Rita Payne who would be the subject of an article on mixed marriage and Rachael would write it. Here is a lady born in Assam, North East India just after Independence was declared in 1947 and where society was still heavily intermingled with British citizens who had chosen to stay and work in the country. Rita was raised in this air and as a child has vivid memories of life at home, the fact that as her father was the first Indian political officer in the North East Frontier Agency meant there were cannons in their front garden with a flag pole. This flag would have been hoisted up when her father was in residence and lowered when he was travelling with the family guarded by Gurkha soldiers known as the Assam Rifles throughout the day and night. Such things would be embedded in a child's mind.

Vivid memories as the only Indian child at children's parties was something which never concerned her and when the time came she was to be enrolled in a Loreto Convent boarding school.

So from Loreto in Shillong to Loreto in Darjeeling, Rita would earn her an MA in English at Delhi University.

This is the point at which this forthright woman believes that coincidence and fate stepped up.

On a visit to Delhi with her father and an arranged meeting with the Director General of All India Radio 1, Rita without any expectation happened to speak briefly to him as they were leaving. Fortuitously she made such an impression that he invited her to audition in voice tests, up against 100 other hopefuls, the outcome being she landed her first job as a presenter and music announcer. That was the first step of fate.

By this time she is 22 years old. She is a high spirited young lady ready for a challenge.

Fate steps up for a second time. Naturally the young damsel hit the social scene and within a short time she was dating a young British architect who was in India for six months on a Commonwealth Scholarship. When his placement finished and he was due to return to Britain they had the choice to never see each other again or get married.

So love won, not up for discussion.

Another time and place, the announcement the same.

Parents have to be told. Rita was an only child from a highly respected family and to her mother and father this was a scandalous situation. Although the decision would not change they would reach a compromise and this time, the parents saw their daughter make her vows agreeing to a traditional Hindu wedding and a three-day ceremony. Much as they so wanted their daughter to stay close, Rita and her new husband flew to Britain in December 1971 leaving behind her glorious life in India to begin their new life together.

That was a culture shock for Rita, except the future held lustre.

Married life commenced and love would deepen in commitment while Rita's husband would continue to follow his career in architecture, they would celebrate the birth of their daughter while living in Istanbul and she herself would move into freelance journalism.

This is the point where her career took off, launched by fashion it seems.

On a whim Rita answered a 'Bride of the Decade', *Cosmopolitan* competition with no expectation. Yet within two weeks her story was announced as the winner and a two-day all expenses second honeymoon to Paris came their way.

The BBC would beckon, Rita was finally on her way, her topics now politics and socialism, 30 years ongoing.

Rita chose love, as did my grandmother Neska.

Israel the Promised Land for Some.

ASHKENAZI EYES

11TH SEPTEMBER 2001 World Trade Centre New York, Twin Towers.

The world stood still, shook to the core by a merciless terrorist attack. This was the face of warfare in the twenty-first century.

Life was to change for everyone in the aftermath and in the midst of high alert and the first official warning after Sept 11, having just presented a series of high-profile international catwalk shows in Excel London, I stepped onto a plane destined for Dallas USA.

A plane carrying only about eight passengers along with airline staff. To be honest I took advantage of the cheap fares. However in the real world fear and suspicion hung in the air.

Walking through Heathrow airport bemused by the lack of travellers suddenly a camera crew approached.

"Excuse us Miss, how do you feel about air travel after the recent terrorist attacks, are you anxious, will it stop you flying?"

Looking slightly distracted at the reporter and without hesitation I spoke.

"I'm from N. Ireland. We've lived with terrorism for over 25 years, we are used to this! They have never stopped me in my life and they are not going to stop me now. They can't be allowed to win."

Thinking back on an entire youth lived in the middle of conflict and unrest, fear and division became a way of life. A quarter of a century in the midst of it. A life somewhat a repeat of the previous century.

Except according to my most favoured pastime back then, fortune tellers I had indeed stared death in the face. That day on York Street when I had walked into the soldier's line of sight by chance. Our days of frayed nerves.

1904 EDITH LEPAR LEOPOLD BORN IN BELFAST
OCT 2001 DALLAS USA
RICHARD LEOPOLD HOUSEHOLD

In the distance I could see Richard, or Dickie as he was affectionately known, and his partner Stephen waving animatedly as I walked through customs into arrivals. Dickie could see a future for me in the USA, he would lay the foundations.

With the roof down of his convertible we drove out to their beautiful home in the suburbs in the balmy late afternoon sunset, the befitting soundtrack of Israel Kamakawiwo'ole serenading us.

Dickie and I, although two different generations are kindred spirits happy to chase rainbows.

So let me introduce the last of the Leopold daughters, Edith. As a young woman she got the opportunity to travel and the USA beckoned. There she was introduced to Raymond Spike, also Jewish and after a short courtship these two lovebirds got engaged. When they made it official with her father and mother's blessing she settled in Cleveland Ohio with her new husband. There they worked hard to build a good life and went on to have a son and a daughter. Dickie was their much-adored son who completed their happiness along with his older sister Norma.

Edith always kept in contact with her Belfast family sending parcels regularly of clothes her children had grown out of amongst other presents and when the special occasion arose she made a couple of transatlantic trips home for family occasions. Beryl often recalls her Auntie Edie stepping in when Auntie Bea thought it was not appropriate for her to be attending a ballroom dance in Belfast and said of course she should go to the Ball, while offering the choice of her own evening jewellery for her niece to wear. American life suited Edith.

Everyone fussed over her son Dickie, he was a worshipped Jewish prince who so adored his Irish connections just as Americans do.

Dickie led a charmed life working in various jobs eventually finding his greatest love in the beauty business and securing employment in the New

York headquarters of one of the grand dames of the beauty business, Madam Helena Rubinstein.

This radical philanthropic woman took the beauty business by storm becoming one of the richest women in the world, opening her first salon in 1915 in New York and leaving a legacy within the cosmetic business to this day. Her charitable Foundation would also donate close to $130 million over 60 years for amongst other things education programmes across the age spectrum, support for the arts and health initiatives and direct services for low income families.

Dickie loved Madam. No job could have been more suited to him. He was this gorgeous young man with a beautiful complexion, a charming asset working in what was to be the city's last decade of mid-century glory. New York in the 1960s was full of life and diversity from the high earners of Madison Avenue to the bohemian artists of the East Village, yet with sinister stealth, social and political unrest, intrigue and organised crime was progressively rupturing life in the city. Chillingly this time of turmoil hovered disastrously on the cusp of violent recession.

22ND NOVEMBER 1963
WORLD NEWS PRESENTED SURREAL HEADLINES.

President John F. Kennedy has been assassinated.

From the USA to The United Kingdom from Germany to Russia the world shook with disbelief.

Everyone had their story of where they were when the news broke.

"Tell me again Dickie, who was there?"

"Well like everyone else I was reeling from the news that our President JFK had been assassinated! When Madam telephoned me and said, 'Wadda you doin tonight? Come and partner me for a game of bridge at my place."

Madam Helena Rubinstein.

"So yes, the night JFK died, I played bridge with Madam and Salvador Dali at her Park Avenue apartment."

Dickie just smiled wryly, nodding his head and remembering this surreal occasion.

As the car slowly parked up in the drive, its occupants were now happy to live in the moment.

"So good to have you here with us." Dickie, USA purveyor of family ties and connections raised his glass to toast his guests at dinner. On the list by Invitation introductions are made.

'SERENDIPITY.'

Top of the list granddaughter of Michael Lepar; Philip's older brother from Kriukai; Guita Schyfter, a tour de force from Mexico, hugely successful in the film industry; and Geraldine Connon, fashionista and a tour de force from N. Ireland always ready for challenge meet for the first time. How was dinner going to pan out Dickie diplomatically observed?

It would turn out to be a battle of wits.

After initial explanations of family ties and connections the talk moved to family skills.

"Explain to me what you do!" Guita says

"I tailor clothes on the cut of the body, it has all to be about proportion, cut and cloth. Then I can be sure it fits and it suits. It's hard to explain, so best I show you. Dickie, let's go to Walmart."

And so we did. After purchasing a couple of plain tablecloths downtown and we got back to the condo, I turned the kitchen into my cutting room, improvising by using the kitchen floor (not for the first time in my career), to cut out the pattern. I then proceeded to pin and fit a twalle onto Guita's frame. Madam stood in silence, I knew my reputation was at stake.

This is my greatest strength, dressing the personality of my client, no pattern required. No lady wants a tape measure run around her.

My favourite saying and criticism of poor design is as the honesty of the child exclaiming, "The King wore no clothes."

In the early years of work there was never the luxury of time to cut paper patterns. As it happens my inherent skill will die with me as it did with Philip. Such technical means would have killed the art in me.

What started as a necessity became the norm. It's all in the eye.

Back in Heathrow Airport as I walked off, I heard a voice saying, "Excuse me, excuse me ", looking round inquisitively at the reporter.

"Wonder could you say that again, it's just you were standing in front of McDonald's last time."

MARCH 2002 NEW YORK

Guita takes delivery of a large Shamrock covered gift box, outfit enclosed.

This was St Patrick's weekend in New York, a double celebration with her film premiere of "*The Faces of the Moon* Guggenheim Museum. Guita Schyfter.

September 2002 London Spanish Film Festival

Walking down Regent Street, London savouring the atmosphere of the city, a little bit anxious to meet Guita again after just a few months previously since dinner in Dallas I suddenly caught a glimpse of her approaching on the same side of the street! Guita seemed entranced by the footpath and the closer she came the more she stared at the ground. She began to circle me as I turned around on the spot, still trying to quietly catch her eye.

"Guita, do you not recognise me?"

"Geraldine, my God I was so busy looking at your shoes. In fact I was going to stop you and ask where you got them? I used to have a pair just like them."

As we let go of our embrace she reached over a gift into my hand.

"For you for making me such a beautiful outfit."

Slightly taken aback, I hesitated, "Oh, thank you, I was not expecting that!"

So as we meandered down Regent Street, I opened the gold embellished box.

Guita smiling proudly, clasped a beautiful Egyptian pearl and jade necklace around my neck.

Theatre, coffee, cake and introductions: as the specially invited guests flurried around the main creator of the night all the ladies took their seats for the film.

"Why did I wear these bloody shoes, they are killing me!"

I wailed in agony in my head.

Suddenly I had an epiphany and moved the ankle elastic over the heels just as they had been left on the shelf at home when I had lifted them down and put them into my suitcase the previous day. How could I have forgotten that pain?

Shoes, shoes, shoes.

RUSSIAN TEA ROOMS @ THE V&A
THE FOLLOWING DAY

The clink of chinaware and the chatter of afternoon tea at the V&A was the perfect setting to celebrate the success of the film. Unexpectedly valuable time together. Guita would pass the remark, "When I met you in Dallas I suspected you to be a spoiled Jewish princess! "

I just smiled realising that was her way of asking for forgiveness for her sharp words about my Catholic grandfather Tommy and getting the point that this spirited untamed woman thrived on reactions.

Enjoying air filled with delicious aromas of all sorts of delicacies infused with all sorts of ornamental teas and the scent of freshly cut flowers.

"Wow you do realise your eyes are the same colour?" the remark was passed.

Once again we nodded in silence at each other, it took a stranger to point out the obvious.

2002-04 THOMAS DUNNE SOCIETY ROSTREVOR CO. DOWN

Who does not love the opportunity to dress up? Certainly not the norm for serious people even at Halloween or the odd murder mystery party. Not the case during the first week of August when in Rostrevor on the formation of the Thomas Dunne Society over twenty years ago by composer, historian and art director Siubhán Ó Dubháin, the Annual Dinner Gala Re-Enactment Event gathers the great and good of high-profile speakers from politics, business and the arts all well attired in the garb of the late 1700s.

The evening celebrates the embodiment of fraternity in United Irishmen and is the finale of a week-long Festival of Culture, music and literature.

The pleasure of listening to the humour and intellect of Sir George Quigley, a top civil servant and business director and advocate of mutual respect in the building of a cohesive shared society could only be matched with the generous spirit, vision and humanity of John Hume – but then enter the room James B King former advisor to Bill Clinton President of the USA.

FOR THE LOVE OF THE IRISH

True to form it was already an evening to remember and as dinner was coming to a close James moved down the room circulating and enjoying the ambiance enthralled by the costumed clad revellers.

Having been introduced earlier, conversation struck up again.

"You know I read palms!" he said to me quite unexpectedly.

How strange I thought, where did that come from? Without hesitation I reached out my hand. Now this party is starting I thought to myself.

"Wow, my goodness I cannot believe what I see in your hand and what I see when I look at you in front of me!" – JBK

Dumbstruck as I waited for his explanation, we were surrounded by eager upturned hands! "Read me, read me!"

After a momentary retreat as I watched the play for his attention and just as he was about to move on, I mustered up the nerve to say, "Oh my goodness, you can't say something like that to me and then not tell me what you see!"

Relieved to recapture his attention. I had my hand outstretched in an instant, saying to myself, he is wearing a suit, he has something to tell me.

"Most people's inner core is fixed, as I say, on a spike. They can move slightly forward or back but that's it. To me YOU are on a swivel, you could go anywhere, anywhere in the world! But... until you can stand in front of the mirror and like yourself... you are going nowhere!" – JBK

SELF

MIRROR MIRROR talk to me
Tell me, tell me what you see
Keep my secret hidden fears
Hold my nerve conceal my tears
Strength is mine let peace prevail
Fail me not nor let me fail

– Geraldine Connon

2011 LINEN MUSEUM LISBURN
'ART IN LINEN' BOOK LAUNCH PRESENTATION

IRISH PEOPLE IRISH LINEN by Kathleen Curtis Wilson

Early 2002 I was introduced to an American writer Kathleen Wilson, a passionate researcher and advocate of the history of Irish Linen.

It was just on my return from Paris and the launch of a new innovative Linen/Lycra cloth. Professor Hill from the Ulster University and former senior tutor of mine had enlisted me to design a Capsule Collection for an Event at the British Ambassador's Residence on Rue du Faubourg Saint-Honoré. It had been his life's work and ambition. A cloth to compete with denim, Linen mixed with Lycra.

The success of the presentation was fortuitous and back in Belfast, Kathleen extended an invitation to me to design a Collection for a Linen Exhibition to be launched in Washington USA and presented in the Smithsonian National Museum of Natural History.

Despite only a few days grace and to affirm my commitment to the project we agreed that I would design a couple of bespoke pieces of clothing for Kathleen. When I delivered them to her hotel and we decided to seal the deal with dinner I found I could eat nothing. Excusing myself from the table I climbed three floors on a spiral staircase only to frantically push the door to the ladies open, run to a cubicle to within a second of an imminent fiasco and took a hit of irrational projectile vomit.

What was that all about I thought? Seemingly a hiatus hernia. Never mind, I had sealed a deal and would never eat Caesar salad again.

Then the Iraq war broke out the following year and my efforts were lost. For the first time in my career conflict won, all funding was suspended and the exhibition would never happen.

Imagine my surprise when virtually nine years later Kathleen emailed out of the blue with an offer I would not refuse. On completing a book on Irish Linen much to my surprise she chose to generously include a chapter on the GC label. Hence when it was to finally hit the shelves, New York,

Washington and Lisburn were in my sights as my invitation to the book launches arrived at my studio.

Fatefully as I searched available hotel accommodation in New York, it fell further and further away from the Irish Embassy, so Washington won.

Somewhere I would never have chosen to visit but thought why not.

With great anticipation along with my compatriot Gerardine we boarded a plane for the USA. I no longer have joy in travelling alone.

Sure the whole trip was exceptional, the elegant architecture of the city, the history, the welcome, the actual event and yet something else of great fortune might be possible.

How could I not do it? As our return flights gave us at least four hours to kill a blissful opportunity of such anticipation fell into our hands, we were to have dinner with Dickie and Stephen in New Jersey. The rendezvous?

Well the airport lounge of course. Oh so clever, oh so special to us.

Imagine our shock when we arrived at the airport to find that we were actually flying out from a sister airport! Miles away!

Any wonder there was so much time! It called for a taxi ride from one suburb of New York to another over an hour and a half away.

It was stomach churning as my precious time ticked away, yet the inner street views of the Bronx and the fast pace of traffic running alongside the Hudson River were intoxicating. As if we were in a movie.

When we finally grabbed our suitcases from the boot of the yellow cab and made our way into the airport none of my telephone calls to Dickie were answered. It had every sign of a lost opportunity.

Resigned that the chance was missed, Gerardine and I cleared security and followed the meandering path of travellers through departures.

None of the shops held any interest for me in my despondency and then. Was that my name? over the tannoy, being repeated a couple of times.

"Listen Gerardine, listen, we need to go back to security."

Just a bit nervous of the reason as we made our way up to a guard, suddenly my heart smiled as I caught sight in the distance of Dickie and Stephen remonstrating to airport staff about their cousin's whereabouts. It was Stephen and I who caught each other's eyes first as the entire airport staff nearly gave us a round of applause. No fancy dinner, no time, just about 40 precious minutes huddled close together in a takeaway diner. Nothing more priceless for Dickie and myself, always wondering if this would be our last meeting.

Within the month Kathleen was in Ireland on her book launch tour.

We would all gather in the Linen Museum in Lisburn.

Three guest speakers were booked for the evening.

Kathleen Curtis Wilson USA author.

Shirley Lord Rosenthal, former Beauty Editor of *American Vogue*.

Geraldine Connon Designer 'Art in Linen' catwalk fashion presentation.

Kathleen and Shirley Lord Rosenthall were the main speakers of the evening, for my part I catwalked a specially designed Linen Collection.

AFTER SHOW RECEPTION

"Whatever happened to the Linen industry in N. Ireland?", lamented a senior civil servant in conversation with a former mill owner.

Whatever indeed!

The Linen Industry's eventual fate lay in the hands of the largest industrialists, mill owners and politicians, both in the UK, Europe and the USA. At the risk of repeating myself the manufacturing process of linen from flax to yarn then cloth took centre stage in N. Ireland, the highest production recorded in the 1920s and yet again I need to say in addition that remarkably, the Belfast York Street Linen Mill employed 5000 workers, the largest in the world at that time.

Overall economies had suffered globally as a consequence of WWI, The League of Nations failed to deliver on its core principles and with increasing poverty and dissent in Germany the German people reacted to what they felt were unfair terms of Treaty of Versailles for them and elected Adolf Hitler as their Chancellor.

The rest is now our history.

With the greatest respect even as the Global Depression began at the end of that decade history records that N. Ireland working classes produced 200,000,000 yards of Linen as part of WWII war effort. United in a common bond the common man delivered for his fellow man to protect their way of life. That was the only power struggle relevant for that moment.

THE ART OF SPREZZATURA
(THE ABILITY OF AN ARTIST TO HIDE THEIR TOIL.)

Oct 2006

So an anniversary was approaching and with no other responsibilities such as children I thought, "It would be good to do something to celebrate 21 years in business. I'm sure we could make it happen. Something worthwhile and I say 'Children in Need'. Time to call in favours I believe!" And so the plan was put in place.

With my team the plan for the anniversary show kicked off. Braced for inevitable madness.

Six weeks of planning, Collections, venue, models, guests, makeup, music, sound, lights, tickets, wine, canopies, seating, programme, rehearsals and everything else that goes with it.

Venue, the renowned Europa Hotel Belfast famous for being the most bombed hotel in the world.

Step up a tight circle of friends. All coming from the light, the shadows behind us no room for egos. Still it was an undertaking, the public eye is sharp and reputation is always at stake.

"Stay calm, it will all be over soon," I said to myself. Think of the cause.

My internal voice however was screaming yet again. What cause?

The demonic clutch which is the fashion scene.

"Why do you keep setting yourself up, why do you need to do this to yourself? This has to be the last time. Stop this madness."

The Europa Show rose to the challenge, only to be expected.

This was the pattern repeated Show after Show, PR campaign after PR campaign, Trade Fair after Trade Fair, year in year out by this time 21 years. The only outcome acceptable was success. From London to Dublin, Paris to Hong Kong. It was always the same.

"Why do you feel the need to push the world in front of you Geraldine, it's not healthy?" Kathleen (Uncle Daniel's wife) pleaded.

"I don't know why, I don't know what drives me and I don't know why

I keep on with it. It's like a disease that's got a hold of me," was my evasive response. But secretly I know.

Likewise my other half would frequently ask, "What's going on in that head now?"

Remembering a trip to an auction one time many years previously with Kathleen and Danny the words would never leave me, "If I was you, I would take it as far as I could go with it."

Uncle Danny had interjected in the course of the conversation in the car. He knew how to strike a chord and he knew his opinion would hit home. Heightened even though I hesitate to suggest magnified by my own merciless Catholic guilt of not wasting a God-given talent. Surely it is better to be occupied of mind and to top that I am that Catholic Jew.

Another memory from that day was my wealthy uncle's elation and eagerness to get me a coffee while we were in Macro, a local food and drink wholesalers. Why? Because it was free!

REHEARSAL AND BACKSTAGE PREP

Rails and rails of clothes from daywear, evening-wear, cocktail, avant-garde. Mountains of shoes of course and hats galore.

A selected party of private clients stepped lightly with excitement through the Collections, charmed to be included in a hushed preview.

Always when you least expect it a breath of fresh air can pass by.

"Come to you see these clothes, did you ever see the like of it?" said a client to her husband.

"Who did you tell me your great-grandfather was?" her husband said to me.

"You know I met him? I was in his factory with my own father. We too manufactured gent's suits, only with us it was for mass production.

"However, we would have sent him special clients who needed bespoke suits. In those days he charged a guinea. We sometimes used to make part payment with silk linings folded to the size of a wallet in a jacket breast pocket and smuggled over the border from down South."

He faltered in his conversation smiling then as if reliving this gambit with satisfaction and humour.

"Amazing! I come from a different background in the trade but whatever it is you are doing and wherever you want to go with this, keep doing it!" David Logan boomed assuredly.

Smuggling indeed I thought, imagine that!

This was I thought a little bit of insight I could surprise my mother with.

Not so it seems, she not only knew about it for she was a smuggler too.

Actually she and all of her aunts worked the railways. Charming.

So it is not all about tailors then, I come from a family of smugglers too.

The manner of her statement was as follows. Just as a matter of fact when I relayed David's confession, she proclaimed that very often when Auntie Bea and she took a day trip to Dublin on the train it was she who always carried the suitcase through customs as the guards would never have questioned her innocent face.

Not so funny on another occasion when Bea and Neska made the run to Dublin. On their return when the guards found a half empty box of cigars in Bea's luggage, they marched Neska off to a side room and strip searched her looking for the rest of them. Of course sister Peggy who was a law unto herself had taken them out for her husband Mac but never thought to mention that.

According to Beryl, if Neska in her hurt and humiliation had gotten the hold of darling Peggy she would have strangled her. The Belfast sisters were incensed even more so when they relayed the story to Minka (Millie).

Any wonder as personalities and relationships changed over time Peggy was best kept living a good hundred miles away.

Even worse! My darling mother who never talks out of turn then reveals the Fermanagh aunts wore smugglers dresses which Tommy's sister May made. The guards or water rats as they were known on their route back from a day out in Bundoran or Pettigo would have waved them across the border remarking, "Well now girls, you are all well improved!"

My mind thinks back to my gorgeous client Barbara and her son inheriting his father's farming skills, surely they weren't participating?

Oh yes for course they were, I recalled my uncle Danny full of admiration for him alongside a Connon cousin smuggling livestock over the border. His admiration fell at my client's husband's feet who displaying no fear would have freely herded their ill-gotten gains right up the middle of Ballymena's main streets. The Connon cousin preferring to slip between pedestrians on the footpaths hiding under his cap.

Danny never admitted to any such activities to me yet my research reveals during WWII if you were not doing it someone in your family was and for sure your friends were. From every walk of life for whatever supplies were needed. Over secluded country roads in all hours of the night or blatantly taking chances at the border on buses, trains and cars claiming "Nothing to Declare".

The Black Market in Ireland escalated, the government was enraged.

2011 HILLSBOROUGH CASTLE
SAVE THE CHILDREN

Charity Fashion Show

Between July 2011 and mid-2012 a severe drought affected the entire region of East Africa. The worst in 60 years, the drought caused an extreme food crisis across Somalia, Djibouti, Ethiopia and Kenya which threatened the lives of 9.5 million.

The awesome committee ladies of Save the Children in N. Ireland rose to the challenge with their fundraising efforts.

A Fashion Spectacular was suggested amongst other events and I have to say even the ladies of the committee could not have envisaged how this show would play out.

With special permission the N. Ireland residence of HM the Queen was secured and plans were put in place. Roll on.

Nothing frivolous levied at the fashion business by the end of that day with £20,000 reached into the coffers of the Charity.

GC Diary

I relished this opportunity.

The effort landed me in A&E not for the first or last time with this job of my own choosing.

He walked into my workshop again. Philip that is.

This time in the guise of a machine technician from Sandy Row, Belfast, a gentleman of the old days, Joe Cully.

Three days before the show my sewing machine packed in and after a few frantic phone calls as arranged he arrived, my mechanic that is, armed with tools. I remember his surprise when he came in, not expecting or believing someone ran a tailoring business in Larne.

Collectively as it turned out we both knew many people from the past in the rag trade. Difference being he knew some who belonged to me, in a time when they sat cross legged on a table.

I hesitated in conversation when he said he knew my great-grandfather.

Looking at this fresh faced gentleman that did not seem at all possible.

He recognised my change of tone and then felt obliged to tell me that he was in fact 79 years of age. That I could hardly believe as I watched and listened to him.

Apart from being greatly impressed that he had not retired it all made sense then.

Delighted and animated to tell me as a young 16-year-old apprentice he had accompanied his boss to the factory on Upper Donegal Street in Belfast. His face lit up with a broad honest smile as he recalled meeting my great-grandfather, looking at me strangely. How could this be?

"Your great-grandfather was looking to buy a buttonhole machine."

"Was he now?" I smiled to myself, something I had always wanted but could never justify.

"Hello Philip, are you looking after me?" I smiled to myself with a wish.

Despite the harshness and rivalry of the rag trade, those in it understand the workings of it.

Mechanics hold their place well.

When I first started in business my mechanic came from the local Mourne Clothing Company in Larne.

He was an angel, Mr Alex Tyrell. A diminutive gentleman, retired when we crossed paths not of course from the workings of sewing machines and the like.

I would collect him at 7pm, he would work until 10 pm and on leaving him home I would ask, "How much do I owe you Mr Tryell?" and he looked straight ahead unflinching and would adamantly say, "That will be £2.50, dear!"

We were, all of us, guilty of undervaluing our skills, God forbid you would get ahead of yourself. It's Larne after all, not Paris. Back then too, Mrs Rainey, our neighbour who perfected many garments for my clients with her beautiful stitching, would often shake her head and remark,

"Geraldine, you make me tired just listening to what you say you need to do." She wouldn't be the first to tell me to stop talking!

2014 STORMONT PARLIAMENT BUILDINGS
GC 30 YEAR ANNIVERSARY SHOW
FOR THE LOVE OF FASHION

Now would I let this go by or not?

Here I am enjoying myself at a wedding and a politician sits down beside me, offering to host a show for me. My immediate thought was "Get thee behind me" and then I regained my manners. So pleasant, not to mention beautifully dressed as she was, I agreed to think about it.

Sometimes it is possible to deliberate too much, nevertheless a decision was taken.

"This Show isn't happening, Stormont is on the verge of collapse, again."

I believe was the comment passed by a client's husband as they prepared to leave their house for Belfast and Parliament Buildings.

Here we go again, Show Time. Along with my 58 strong creative team working silently in side rooms and the corridors of the contentious seat of N. Ireland, politics, disquietude simmered within our ranks as if in limbo.

The unexpected invitation now having been taken up would see my plans and organisation skills suffocating in protocol. It was a nightmare.

With one day to go the pressure was taking its toll, the walls were caving in! As I ran last minute errands I came across Davy Robinson, a well-known local character who had worked a thousand years ago for my Uncle Danny.

Distracted with the fast-approaching deadlines, I was tempted to run past him as he was bending down to pick up something on the ground, it would have been so easy to have slipped by him unnoticed. However, as if something or someone made me, I stopped in front of him.

"How are you Davy?" Looking up he replied, "Ah it's yourself. I hear you're doin' a BIG SHOWWW!"

"Mmmm, I am," I smiled,

Davy always made me smile with his exaggerated dramatic take on all things!

"You'll get a free meal up there," he suggested.

"Not a chance Davy, not even a biscuit!" Amused as always.

Then without warning with his countrified jacked up drawl he leaned in close and whispered under his voice… as if knowingly.

"Danny will be luckin down on ye!" He smiled and winked.

What a divine possibility.

"Good to see you, Davy. I'll hold that thought." as I looked up to the sky.

DEC 3rd 2014 'For the Love of Fashion', Stormont Parliament Buildings.

DEC 2nd 2014 Guita Schyfter arrived from Mexico into London premiering her latest film, and the same day Beryl Connon turned 83 years of age.

THE ARTS & ARTISTS IN N. IRELAND

2016 CAMERATA Music Festival, Clandeboye Estate, County Down.

Music inevitably is the soundtrack to life and when your path crosses people, certain ones make a bigger impression than others.

I can pinpoint exactly when I fell in love with classical music. It was as I watched *Schindler's List* at the cinema, my heart became swept up in it.

From then it was my favoured choice of music for sending models down the catwalk or playing late into the night, alone in my workshop studio.

Strangely on a visit to Hungary one time I remember listening in awe to a quartet playing a haunting piece of music from the bastion of Matthias Church on the Buda side of Budapest overlooking the Danube and following a tour of Pest and the history of the region during WWII.

No more beautiful music fits or echoes better the cast of emotions endured in the ugliness of war.

As for people who make a mark on you, Barry Douglas CBE is one of these people, an exceptional world-renowned pianist who has carved out a notable career in classical music since winning the Gold Medal at the Tchaikovsky International Piano Competition in Moscow.

In 1997 he founded the chamber orchestra Camerata Ireland to nurture, encourage and celebrate the very best of young musicians from both the North and South of Ireland striving for musical excellence and at the same time aiming to further the peace process in Ireland by promoting dialogue and collaboration through its education programmes.

Ireland once was described as the land of saints and scholars, not many saints these days, excluding my mother, however, creatives are on the move up and under the umbrella of this embodiment of creativity, Barry has also embraced the field of fashion working exclusively with one of N. Ireland's true fashion doyen's, Maureen Martin, who herself can claim rights to the bespoke tailors of the past when her own mother, a highly qualified seamstress worked in the height of the trade in the 1930s in the city.

Maureen's talent lies in PR, Model Management and high-profile fashion events. A career which began in London when she was photographed by the then latest photographer on the block, David Bailey.

Maureen thought nothing of it or him surprisingly back then. However as his fate played out and luck opened doors he, along with Terence Donovan and Brian Duffy happened to be in the right place at the right time, capturing and helping to create the Swinging London of the 60s.

Just as a matter of interest these three photographers were elevated to celebrity status socialising with actors, musicians and royalty, earning a laudatory title from London's resident god-father of photography Norman Parkinson when he named them 'The Black Trinity'.

Maureen herself, ever swept up in the glamour became a member of the Film Artists Association appearing in numerous films until inevitably she found her direction, it was to be in fashion and for 40 years she has never swayed from it. That crazy cult we belong to.

Her passion is the promotion of young design talent, a determination she has followed faithfully on the Style Council of the UK and Ireland working with designers such as Roland Mouret, Matthew Williamson, Alexander McQueen, John Rocha, Vivienne Westwood and the artisan that is Zandra Rhodes.

In the realms of work not everyone is cut out to be a civil servant, accountant, bank manager or in more familiar words tinker, tailor, soldier, sailor, rich man, poor man, and sadly even beggar man.

Anyhow with Maureen in mind one of the most memorable events she produced on N. Ireland turf was for Givenchy, a French luxury fashion and perfume house. It was founded in 1959 (the year I was born) in Paris and is a member of Chambre Syndicale de La Haute Couture and Pret-a-Porter.

On this occasion, the guest star of the catwalk was French model and actress Capucine, famous for her role in the iconic film, *The Pink Panther*.

In the audience and very special guest of honour was philanthropist Sacha Hamilton, the Duchess of Abercorn, watching with such pleasure as willowy models sashayed down the catwalk wearing the latest Collection of beautifully created ensembles.

Any student who shared the catwalk that night could only have been emboldened.

So as it happened and I had drawn the curtain on older collaborations a new door opened.

With the greatest of pleasure I accepted the invitation to show at the fashion event at Camerata beginning in 2015, the theme based on the beauty of opera. This led on to the following year, 2016 and the highly significant festival which marked the 30th anniversary of Barry Douglas's Tchaikovsky Award, even more enjoyable as it was to embrace a strong Russian theme.

2017 then followed with Parisian influence. All was good.

There was great anticipation of all musical performances throughout the week and then the Fashion Show Event arrived. The preparations for it had also reached a high pitch. Rehearsals for the catwalk were completed, featuring young up and coming musicians following lead flautist Eimear McGeown, now well on her way to success.

To all intents and purposes everything and everyone was in place. There was a sense of relief. Backstage we were ready to go.

Strangely then without any notion of trouble there was a request for me to step outside. My thoughts were, my God I do not have time for this.

At this point I am told that Beryl had taken a fall, was on her way to hospital, that she was fine, there was no need for me to worry, but she would not be attending the show. In my head the music stopped.

A dull cloud descended on me as I became very cold. Surely not.

I remember taking the news on board yet a wild calmness set in. Was history coming back to haunt me? I could do nothing else, the news I kept to myself, the show had to go on.

A cracked pelvis and cancer scare would be the diagnosis.

Six weeks later, as we sat in the hospital, slowly recovering from the trauma, Beryl's social worker Mrs Logan introduced herself and our conversation took such a strange twist. Typically a consequence of ill health can feed vulnerability and hope for reassurance, exceptionally that can come in all forms. We would get a clear sign all was fine.

The topic of long work hours was raised and on explaining my business, my dear mother lamented about the hours I kept in work. Mrs Logan reassured us that she knew all about those hours. It was indeed very familiar to her and her mother. Then with no warning or understanding of the connection she announced clearly that in their case, her father had worked in tailoring in Belfast but he worked for Philip Leopold and Son.

Startled, I said, " That's mum's grandfather , my great grandfather!"

In that cold moment eyes wide open, we just glanced hard at each other in disbelief.

"My goodness" exclaimed Mrs Logan

as she rubbed the hair on the back of her arms.

VOGUE HEADQUARTERS; JUNE 1994
LONDON HANOVER SQUARE

As the lift ascended to the first floor the two occupants struck up conversation.

"Gosh I just managed to avoid that downpour of rain."

I chatted away unconcerned. "It came out of nowhere!"

"Me too, talk about unpredictability!" remarked the other lady checking out my style. As the lift doors opened, we smiled broadly to each other and then went in different directions. I approached the reception desk.

"I've an appointment with Jacqueline Euwe 3.20 pm, Geraldine Connon."

Eyes lowered I had hardly sat down to wait, wondering how cold this reception was going to be having experienced the sharpness of Ms Euwe 40 mins earlier. Within seconds of her being alerted she appeared, skipping down the stairs and before even reaching the bottom step announced

"Geraldine, would you like to come up to the office?" JE

"Of course. Thank you!" quite dazed "Wow what's just happened?"

"The lady I want you to see, you were just talking to her in the lift!" JE

That could only be luck and now we two ladies already knew each other having unsuspectedly met five minutes earlier.

"It is a pleasure to meet you Geraldine, your work is outstanding, when you decide which direction you are going to take your business in, let me know."

Her laudatory words echoed around the hushed open-plan office. Was that Joan's plan?

"Now Jaqueline, would you kindly show Geraldine to the escalator."

Stepping into the lift I graciously shook Jacqueline's hand finally and once the door closed, I checked my father's watch, 4 pm.

I had managed it, 40 minutes in conversation with a top *Vogue* editor, not just 10 mins as had been forewarned by Ms Euwe.

Twenty years later after watching a screening of the highly publicised *September Issue A Vogue Insight*, I felt compelled to email Joan Rolls and finally tell her that my decision had been to consolidate and focus on my biggest strength of bespoke tailoring for private clients and now had after all over 35 years and ongoing survived the fashion business.

This gorgeous lady having moved on from her time at *Vogue* now heads up PR for Van Cleef & Arpels International exquisite jewellery.

I smile to myself when I recall how she had admired just with a glance, my broach that day in the lift. A sign of things to come for her.

DECEMBER 2018 GC STUDIO

After a last-minute decision to spend a few days In New York and soak up the Christmas atmosphere of the Big Apple, on my return I thought it best to collect the mail from the studio despite the late hour.

It is a busy time of the year and I wanted no surprises.

Well that is except for the one waiting.

"Read that," I quietly said to my sister Roisin.

"What is it?" Was her nervous reply, "Not bad news I hope!"

"No no, just read it."

Watching intently I stood back.

"Is this for real? It looks authentic!" she spoke quietly, adding, "Well how amazing is that?"

There it was, an invitation to Buckingham Palace.

Presenting the first Commonwealth Fashion Exchange hosted by Catherine, The Duchess of Cambridge; Sophie, The Countess of Essex and Princess Beatrice along with representatives in fashion from the 52 countries of the Commonwealth. Never mind the height of society.

The promise of a colourful evening to say the least. Maybe even the beginning of new things to come as I cast my mind back to the essence of Princess Diana.

Then I smiled wryly to myself, knowing I should harbour no expectations. None.

The setting, well that was a whole different thing. Uncle Danny would have shared my enthusiasm.

FEBRUARY 2018 BUCKINGHAM PALACE

Security is very tight, only to be expected. The traffic around The Mall is an array of agitated tempers. Then civility rolled up as we parked by the Palace railings amidst the style.

The taxi driver opened the door, took my hand and helped me onto the cobbled footpath.

"Enjoy yourself," he smiled warmly.

Walking across the gravel forecourt as it crunched underfoot, each step taking me closer, it was a surreal moment. Isobel, my confidante and friend who generously travelled with me for some company, at least until I got there as it was not a plus one invitation, wished me well.

I steeled myself knowing to many, I would be invisible, as I glanced at the stars twinkling above me.

There in the Picture Gallery as the top contributors to the fashion world mingled with royalty and the elite of society vying for position, I smiled to myself. Silently watching in the background. Or so I thought.

"Turn around, I love what you are wearing, my favourite colour, what a beautiful red, you must be one of the designers?"

I turned to face the most gracious regal Indian lady.

"Let me introduce myself, my name is Rita Payne. I am the President of the Commonwealth Journalists Association and who are you?"

It was like watching a scene from a play. Some ably better actors than others.

Anyhow for my part I watched and chose to wait to be introduced to those and

only those whom others of high position thought I should meet. "And in what capacity are you here this evening?"

CHALLENGE

Ask a child and you will hear their dreams
It makes you smile, what does that mean
Pure in thought , word and deed
Capture that, your soul to feed
Life needs purpose or there is no quest
Look to your strengths, choose the best
Take heed my friends for what comes your way
In the shadows of night or in the cold light of day
Rise above anger and weakness in fools
Rise above hatred, savage and cruel
Love with honesty your passion will shine
Gather wisdom, oh would it be mine
Open your eyes and see what could be
Was that meant for you, was that meant for me
Walk with humility not empty pride
The world is our oyster, side by side
Find a direction and follow it true
Check your conscious, always be you
A You to be proud of, at the end of your day
Know kindness is not weakness as they say
Love with honesty, passion and care
Cherish great moments, they can be rare
Celebrate honesty no greater way
Enjoy your sleep at the end of your day
Come from the light it's good for your heart
Who knows who's watching
We are never apart

– *Geraldine Connon*

This is part of the tale of all my extraordinary ordinary people, for the most already dead.

No one has come back yet to tell us where we are going wrong, even though my Aunt Kathleen promised or actually threatened she would, yet strangely just the other day she smiled at me from a photobooth pic of her, I do not remember ever seeing or collecting, which fell out of a bundle of photographs for some reason.

Beryl listening quietly in the background to my imaginations knows that I believe Philip's energy is all around her.

On numerous occasions over the years while she was hospitalised and vulnerable in passing conversations with carers and staff, they told her they knew and loved her grandfather or one of their family had worked for him. That was a comfort to her being a realist, as she does not need to read anything more into it. Not like her fanciful daughter willing such signs.

"Wasn't that strange?" Beryl would say. "Imagine, they knew my Granda."

30th Jan 2020

"Where will we meet? Lunch near the castle will be great. Sounds good".

Beryl and I sat down with Neill Cranston, the now 81-year-old grandson of Thomas Neill, my great grandfather's barber who answered my research appeal in the *Shankill Mirror*.

He too called my grandfather by his title, Mr Leopold.

It gave us the opportunity to tell him that Thomas was listed as a referee for Philip to secure his British Citizenship in 1925. The significance of which cannot be measured and in turn it gave Neill the chance to bring Philip back to us as he recalled him in his grandfather's barber's shop.

August 2019 Europa Hotel Belfast

While Beryl and my sister Roisin along with her husband Vincent were greeted by the general manager of the Europa Hotel, James McGinn with his usual 'charming' aplomb and seated in the dining room, I waited in the foyer for our guests.

Smiles all around, hands on hearts we all knew who we were when the lift doors opened.

For a very precious few hours only, my family and I dined with Shmuel Lepar's granddaughter Sarah and her husband Zeev Lubratski. Travelling from their home in Israel they too are on a quest to research family ties. In the course of the evening as we reminisced of family, Sarah recalled meeting

Uncle Alec Leopold in South Africa as an elderly man. When the war ended, the workshop closed up and Philip died, his brother Robert brought him and his darling wife Sofie over to Rhodesia. Sarah loved them and told us how she had listened affectionately to his stories about family life in Kriukai. He truly was also a man with a broken heart who at least would spend his final days with his brother and his family. Of course Beryl on the other hand remembers Alec and Sofie in their younger years. Reminiscing that despite living in Dublin they frequently visited the Leopold tailors in Belfast.

So what was Beryl's greatest memory of her uncle?

Well it was that of a young modest girl who braced herself when she saw him coming towards her, smiling with such happiness as he held her head in his hands and kissed her face all around from one side to the other. Such is love.

ACKNOWLEDGMENTS OF CONTRIBUTORS
AND SUPPORTERS

I made the decision I was going to write a book. Why? Too good a story not to write.

The difficulty, in real life I tend to ramble on. No one would have the patience to read it.

The task, tell the short version. I have. However, not without the following people who had to bear with me and my persistence for answers.

When I first began the research I was intrigued by the fact that my great grandfather's personal information was held by law under Freedom of Information rules. That was the start.

Many many conversations later, copious amounts of free time because of the Covid Pandemic, writing into the early hours of the morning, sometimes all night long I have signed off on it.

All these friends old and new along with family, finally can answer my calls and open emails, texts and messages without fear of one topic of conversation. Thank you.

FAMILY

My co writer and mother Beryl (Rolston) Connon, whose strength cannot be measured.

Her sharp memories of family life and in particular her beloved grand-father, delightfully not once in recalling her stories did she flinch or tell it differently than she ever had.

I imagine you have got a flavour of her by now and I should let it go with that yet I am compelled to reveal as our book reached its final stages the unthinkable happened.

6th october 2021 Mum fell and sustained shocking injuries.

The assessment revealed a cut to her forehead needing 9 stitches, a bleed on her brain, broken nose, broken eye socket and cheekbone and finally a broken neck.

She fought for her life still, celebrated her ninetieth year and after three gruelling months arrived home, not ready to leave us on Christmas Eve.

Family members;

Leslie Leopold, Belfast Patriarch of our family. Very long suffering of my calls.

Richard Leopold, USA Patriarch of our family and another hoarder of photographs

Mervyn and Rae Silverstein Australia, Dolly Leopold's grandson

Guita Schyfter, Mexico, Michael Lepar's granddaughter

Sarah and Zeev Lubratzki, Israel Shumel Lepar's granddaughter

Roisin Craig

Vincent Craig

Hannah Craig

Matthew Craig

Brian Connon

Amy Connon and Blaine Mc Keever my computer wizards

Neska Connon

Michael Connon

Angela Connon

Anna Connon

Eva Connon

Amanda (Moss) Rose and Albert Coss's daughter & Simon Jackson, London

Rachael Leopold, Leslie Leopold's daughter

Simon Levy, Dolly Leopold's grandson Australia

Vincent Rolston

Miguel Neves who never doubted my commitment

Private clients for their unwavering support

FRIENDS, AUTHORS and WRITERS

who encouraged, advised and made introductions for me to connect and gather information.

Rita Payne; President Emeritus Commonwealth Press Association

Roland Spottiswoode and Sara Craig Lanier; Ardrigh Books who very kindly took valuable time to proofread my very poor first draft and critiqued it with kindness and encouragement.

Don Bigger; Military Historian who likewise very generously took valuable time out to proofread the second draft; that was a very nervous wait for his opinions, critique and measured direction.

Every question was simply answered throughout a year and a half of "What do you think?"

Norman Houston; Former Director of N.Ireland Office Washington, close friend, confident & proofreader. Now sadly gone much too soon.

Mark Huffam , Film producer who took the time to read and critique a very early manuscript.

Philip Ollerenshaw; An amazing historian, whose research was beyond beneficial to this story, and who, on the very day I tried to contact to confirm his findings, sadly and shockingly died that same day. I wrote to his friend and colleague historian Liam Kennedy QUB to at least offer my sincere condolences to him on his loss of such an esteemed colleague.

The Economic History of Ulster; Philip Ollerenshaw; reference WWII War Effort in N.Ireland

Isobel & Campbell Tweed. Close friends, confidants and partners in crime and adventures.

Eileen Martin Callan, QUB, long time friend, supporter and confidant

Jacqui Kerr; Life coach, long time friend and supporter. Belfast

Fiona Cook; closest confidant. Belfast

Shankill Library; Shankill Road Belfast

Bobby Forrester; North Belfast

John Mc Vicker; Shankill Mirror news editor

Neill Cranston, barber grandson of Thomas Neill, barber and referee for Philip Leopold

Maureen Martin; Maureen Martin Model Agency

Barry Douglas; Camerata Ireland

Jon & Una Lashford and Gerardine Mulvena. Lifes debaters.

Gladys Greer; Greer Publications

Irish Jewish Roots; Stuart Rosenblatt, Dublin

Ben Magrill, Jewish Belfast Forum Facebook

PHOTOGRAPHERS

Joe Mc Kay; Photographic enhancement and film reproduction of all photography

Imagery from Clandeboye Estate and Irish Linen Museum

Darren Kidd; , Kelvin Boyes, Press Eye; Imagery from Hillsborough Castle, Stormont Parliament Buildings

Mitchell Cahoon; Imagery from Clandeboye Estate

Michael Mc Kay; Photograpy

Henri Solomon; Most precious historical family photographs

Malka Coler; Daughter in law of Henri Solomon, California
Shira Bliss; Granddaughter of Henri Solomon, USA
Neil Murry man of patience & photographic team Pharmacy Plus Larne

BOOK COVER
Justin Lashford, Graphic designer and guy also of immense patience.

NEWSPAPER EDITORIALS and OFFICIAL ORGANISATIONS
PRONI, Belfast
National Museums N.Ireland Belfast, Stephen @ Picture library
The National Archives Kew, London
Belfast Telegraph, Archive
British Newspaper Archive, online
American War records, online
Historical research online
Donna Traynor BBC
Laura Mc Daid BBC
Anne Marie McAleese BBC
Gareth Howard CEO Authoright for affording this publication opportunity

11th March 2022. Holding her hand and praying, I placed my other hand on her heart. We stood around Beryl with love until I whispered she's gone, just as I felt her last, blessed beat at 90 years old and she slipped away from us.

Finally I understand the madness of my career. It seems it had always been just for her and Gerry.

Fear tried to come in, swiftly belied by Mervyn Silverstein in Australia on reflection of the anniversary of his own mam Gladys, Dolly Leopold's daughter. He lost her on that same date, 1979, thirty three years earlier. The spirit lives.

Vincent Rolston smiled as he remembered as young cousins, Beryl's favourite phrase,

"You might as well be out of this world, than out of fashion."

I never heard her say it, for life had brought her too many other responsibilities by the time I came to know her. Wish I had known.

IRELAND
THE CHOSEN LAND
FOR
OTHERS

Whispers whispers in my mind
Why not listen they are only kind
Take hold of your challenge, realise your might
If it's Heaven or Hell always look to the light
Understand silence is neither meek or mild
Hold onto your dreams as free as a child

– Geraldine Connon

THE PHOTOGRAPHIC COLLECTION

To my readers

This tells the story visually from beginning to end.
Imagery of people, places and times.
My thought would be that the book should be read first and
then brought to life through the photographs.
By this stage you will already know the personalities and
so you will know them by name.

Geraldine Connon

Every effort has been made to identify owners of copyright.
Any errors or omissions will be corrected in future editions.

Philip Lepar Leopold
The Immigrant Belfast circa 1909

Family photograph

Philip Lepar Leopold and Rose
Patjunski Wedding portrait Belfast 1899

Photographer unknown

Postcard Belfast 1892

BELFAST

16531.

Postcard Belfast 1890s

436-Royal Avenue, N. W. from Donegal Place, most important street
of Belfast, Ireland.   Copyright 1903 by Underwood & Underwood.

Postcard Belfast 1912

all Place, "Belfast.

Cave Hill.

Postcard Belfast 1910 Cavehill

Belfast.

Left to right; Minka (Millie), Edith, Neska, Peggy Leopold dressed in linen and lace circa 1912

Photographer Henri Solomon
Permission of use Malka Coler California USA

Sonny Leopold with his father Philip Leopold circa 1920

Photographer Henri Solomon
Permission of use Malka Coler California USA

Lally, Philip Sonny and Rose Leopold Belfast circa 1925

Photographer Henri Solomon
Permission of use Malka Coler California USA

Beryl Rolston Belfast 1948
Photographer Ashleigh Studios Belfast

Gerry Connon and Beryl Rolston 1955 Engagement Celebration

Family photograph

Gerry Connon 'First and Last Bar' Station Road Larne circa 1953
Family photograph

Brian Connon First born outside his grandparents, Neska and Tommy Rolston's home on the terrace on Bank Road Larne circa 1961

Family photograph

Beryl Connon nee Rolston with her children Brian, Roisin and Geraldine circa 1961 in the back garden of their grandparents home on the Bank Road, Larne

Family photograph

Geraldine Connon in back garden of her grandparents home on the Bank Road, Larne
circa 1961

Family photograph

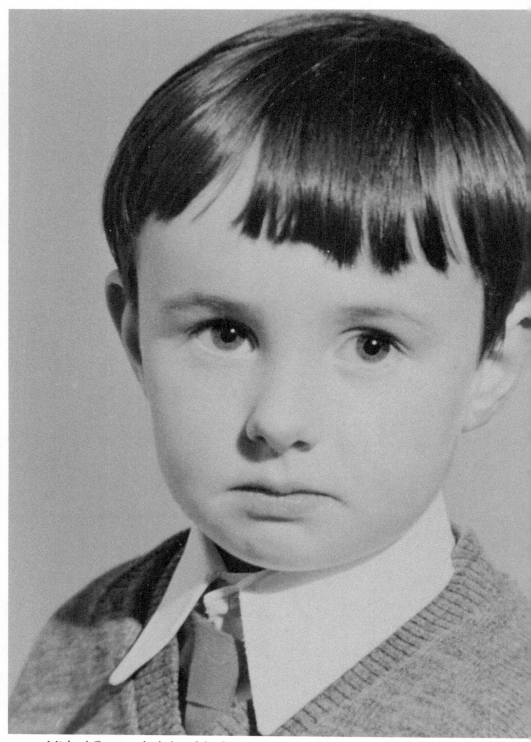

Michael Connon the baby of the family courtesy of St. Anthony's Primary School 1971
Photograph Mr Browne Larne

Kathleen Meehan and Danny Connon Honeymooners in Dublin 1930
Family photograph

Alec Lepar Leopold born 1899 Kriukai
Immigrant who joined his uncle Philip in Belfast and changed his name to Leopold
Enlisted in the North Irish Regiment. Portrait 1918 Belfast

Photographer R Gledhill Bangor

Alec and Sofie Wedding Portrait 10th August 1930

Photographer unknown

Folio............................ Date.....................

....

....

....

PHILIP LEOPOLD,

General Draper and Outfitter

169 Oldpark Road,

BELFAST.

NOTICE.

Please do not ask for any more Goods until first Account is paid, as a refusal often offends.

TO PAY...

H. EVANS PRINTER, 17 PERTH STREET, BELFAST.

Philip Leopold Business order book Front and Back

BUSINESS HOURS

Monday
Tuesday ⎫
Thursday ⎬ 9 a.m. till 7 p.m.

Wednesday, 9 a.m. till 1 p.m.

Friday,   ... 9 a.m. till 8 p.m.

Saturday, ... 9 a.m. till 9-30 p.m.

All Kinds of General Drapery
Goods Supplied.

Thomas Neill and assistant outside his barber shop Courtesy Neill Cranston

Neska Leopold and her cousin attending a wedding in Leeds circa late 1920s Photograph
John Garratt Leeds

Tommy Rolston and Neska Leopold The secret wedding day 1930
Family photograph

Neska Leopold circa 1929 Photographer Henri Solomon

Permission of use Malka Coler California

Thomas Rolston Carnboy Fermanagh
Photographer Josie Rolston

Bea Leopold and Sam Freeman Wedding
Guests and reception Clifton Street Orange Hall Belfast circa 1919

Photographer Henri Solomon
Permission of use Malka Coler California USA

Four generations of Jewish Ancestry living in Belfast circa 1895-1921

Left to right; Rose Patjunski Leopold and her eldest daughter Bea with baby Dorothy
Seated; Rose Patjunski's mother owner of the lodging house where Philip came to stay

Photographer unknown

Edith (Edie) Leopold and Neska Leopold with Dorothy Freeman circa 1932 Belfast

Photographer Henri Solomon
Permission of use Malka Coler California USA

Dolly Leopold Belfast 1920s
Photograph Ashleigh Studios Belfast

Dolly Leopold Wedding portrait March 1926 Belfast

Photographer Henri Solomon
Permission of use Makla Coler California USA

Wedding group photograph 1926 Belfast Left to right;

Alec Leopold, Bea and Sam Leopold, Philip and Rose Leopold, Mrs Cohan, Dolly and Harry, Mr Cohan Sr and Mr Cohan junior, the groom's brother

Photographer Henri Solomon
Permission of use Malka Coler California USA

Dolly Leopold and Harry Cohan Wedding Portrait Left to right;
Patjunskis cousin, sisters Edith, Neska, Harry ,Dolly, Peggy, Minka (Millie)

Photographer Henri Solomon
Permission of use Malka Coler California USA

Sonny Leopold with two friends dressed in the garb of the day Belfast circa 1930s
Family photograph

Philip and Sonny Leopold Belfast circa 1930s
Family photograph

Philip, Bea and Sonny Leopold outside his Drapers Store Belfast circa 1920s Family
photograph

The Leopold sisters dressed in military gabardine
Belfast circa 1915

Left to right;
Minka (Millie), Peggy, Neska, Edith

Photographer Henri Solomon
Permission of use Malka Coler California USA

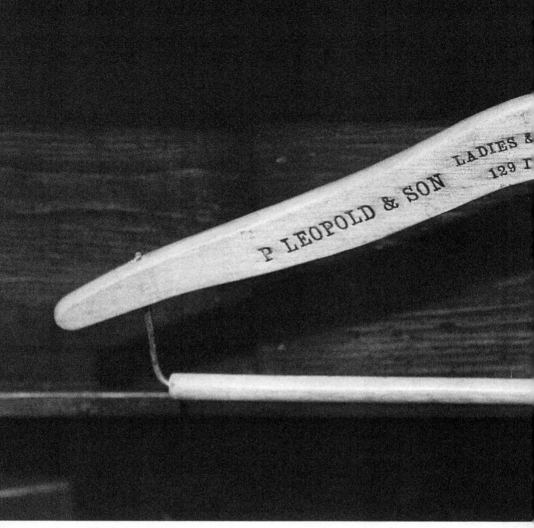

Leopold Clothes Hanger

Photographer Joe McKay Larne

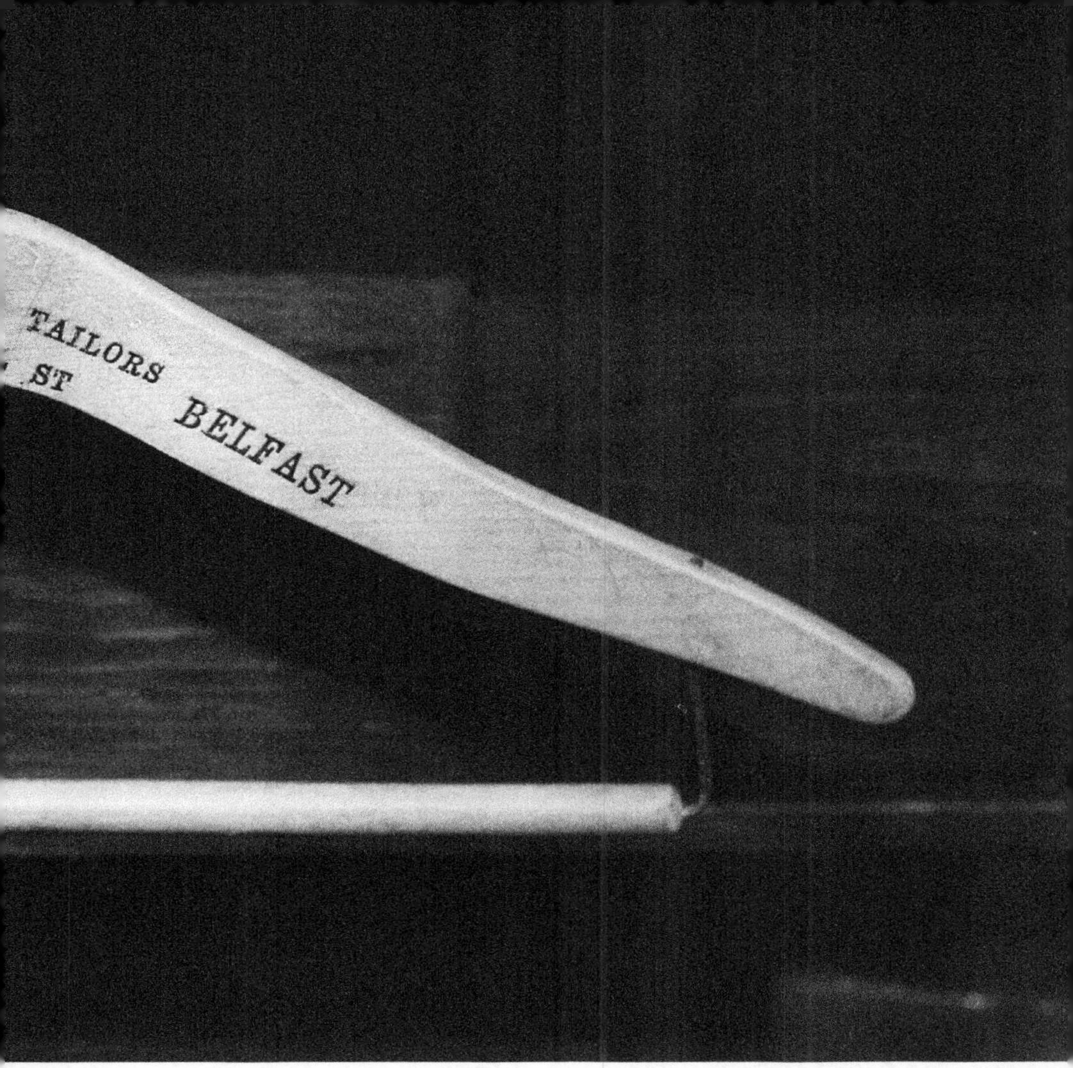
TAILORS
ST
BELFAST

Philip Leopold Belfast circa 1921
Photographer John Garratt Leeds

Geraldine Connon circa 2021
Photographer Mitchell Cahoon

Sam Freeman glass signage from The Elephant Building Belfast 1950s

Photographer Joe McKay Larne

EMAN

ss Tailor

OO3

The Tailors Belfast circa 1926 Left to right
Alec Leopold, Bea Leopold Freeman, Sam Freeman, Philip Leopold

Photographer Henri Solomon
Permission of use Malka Coler California USA

Minka (Millie) Leopold, Albert Coss,
Jacqueline Cohan Wedding Portrait

Belfast 14/6/1933
Photographer Henri Solomon
Permission of use Malka Coler California USA

Philip and Rose Leopold at home in Belfast circa 1934
The last photograph of them, unaware their time together was running out

Family photograph courtesy Amanda Jackson London

Beryl.
Me.

Rose Coss and Beryl Rolston Belfast circa 1948 How Rose adored her big cousin

Family photograph courtesy Amanda Jackson London

Philip and his sister Aunt Alma Belfast circa 1919
Photographer unknown

Neska and Philip with young Leslie, Bea and Sam's son Belfast circa 1920

Family photograph

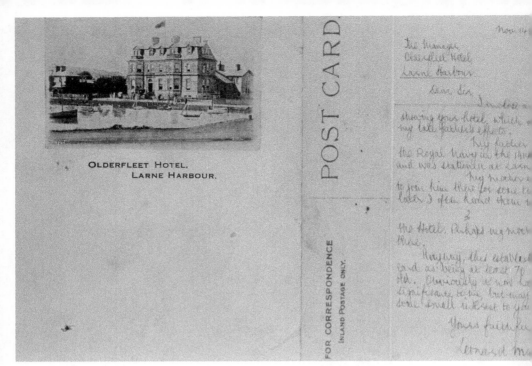

Olderfleet Hotel postcard

Danny Connon as success followed him, would eventually purchase the star of his portfolio. The Olderfleet Hotel at the harbour in Larne. Having worked there as a young bartender when he first moved to the town he had vowed to own the property one day. This is a private letter from an American tourist relaying a time in his own fathers life when he was stationed there during WWII. The hotel had been commissioned by the Government during the War serving as the Allies Naval Headquarters.

WWII Leopold Household Belfast circa 1942-45 Left to right;
Minka (Millie), Rose, Bea, Philip, Jewish soldier and Leopold tailor

Family photograph

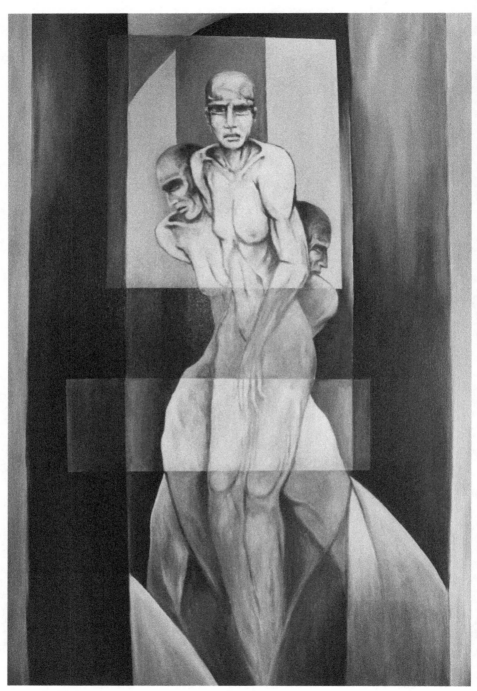

'KAMP' in oils by Jon Lashford

Photograph Joe McKay Larne

Shmuel Yakov, Kriukai Lithuania, circa early 1900s Family
Photograph courtesy Sarah Lubratski Israel

The Girl In The White Dress Kriukai, Lithuania, Circa late 1930s

The extended Lepar Family with their neighbours.

In 1941 the reach of the Nazi's extermination of Jews gathered pace and bled out of control. As the family struck such a picture of unity in life they would all face unity in their final moments. The only survivor was The Girl in the White Dress, Fanny Lepar

Left to right;

Standing; Mussa (married to Efraim Lepar) Laltke Pereztman (the neighbour who was like family), Pesca, Singer, Shoshana (sister of Avi)

Sitting; Efriam Lepar Yankele (son of Mussa & Efriam), Fanny Lepar, (mother of Guita Schyfter film maker) Avi Lepar (brother of Nachum Lepar, father of Sarah Lubratski)

All the way in the background, smiling from a distance hovers Michael Lepar (Philip Leopold's brother)

Photograph courtesy of family Sarah Lubratski, Israel and Guita Schyfter, Mexico City

Michael Lepar with his granddaughter Luba, sister of
Fanny, Guita Schyfter's mother alongside her father
Solomon Schyfter at Luba's brother Max's farm in Costa
Rica Circa 1930s

Family photograph courtesy of Guita Schyfter Mexico
City and Sarah Lubratski Israel

Kriukai Lithuania Circa
1931-1933

Left to right, Top; Fanny Faiga,
Bat Sheva Middle; Chaviva,
Guita, Pesca

Bottom; Nachum Lepar, Bat
Sheva, Chaviva are brother and
sisters

Fanny Lepar is the daughter
of Tsipa and Yehushua Zinger,
mother of Guita Schyfter Mexico
and sister of Pesca

The Guita in the center, is
another relative from Latvia who
visited family in Kriukai

Family Photograph courtesy of
Guita Schyfter Mexico City and
Sarah Lubratski Israel

Rose Coss and her grandfather Philip Leopold Belfast circa 1945

The innocence of Rose dressed in military gabardine is so markedly different to the pain of loss etched on his face

Photograph Henri Solomon
Permission of use Malka Coler California USA

Minka (Millie) Leopold and friend, Summer vacation circa 1930s

Family Photograph

A day out to the beach circa 1920s as written up in Rose Coss diary Inside the car; Sonny Leopold, Sonny Diamond, Bea Leopold, and friend

Outside the car; Mrs Diamond (proprietor of the Jewish butchers Antrim Road Belfast) Rose Leopold in the fox fur, a friend and Millie (Minka) Leopold

Family photograph courtesy Amanada Jackson nee Moss

Later that same day out on the beach
Family photograph

Jewish life in Belfast circa late 1930s

Left to right; two unknown friends, Minka Leopold Coss, Albert Coss, Bea Leopold Freeman with her hands on her beloved son Leslie's shoulders, Sam Freeman, Alec Lepar Leopold and his wife Sofie Baker Leopold

Family photograph

James Rolston Sr. Tommy Rolston's father Carnboy, Fermanagh circa 1930
Family photograph

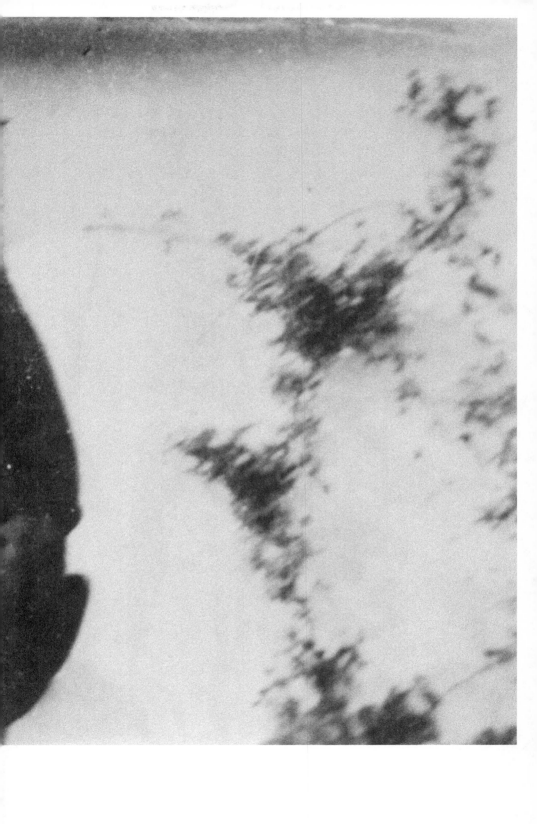

Carnboy Fermanagh circa 1932
Tommy and Beryl Rolston

Family photograph

Summer holidays Ballyferris
Co.Down circa 1933
Tommy and Beryl Rolston

Family photograph

Belfast circa 1932 Neska and Beryl Rolston
Family photograph

Holidays in Donegal circa 1936-37
Minka (Millie) Leopold Coss and her daughter Rose
Family photograph

Belfast circa 1947-49
Rose Coss and Auntie Bea Leopold Freeman

Family photograph

Carnboy Co.Fermanagh circa early 1950s Outside Sissy and Pat Murphy's home
Left to right; Beryl & Gerry Connon, Neska Rolston, Sissy and Pat Murphy

Family photograph

Summer holidays Donegal circa 1940
Beryl Rolston and her grandfather
Philip Leopold

Family photograph

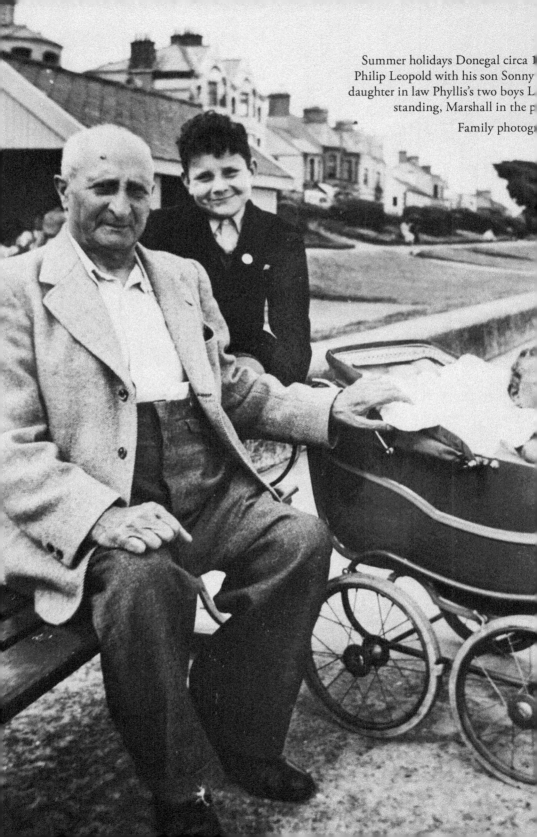

Summer holidays Donegal circa 1
Philip Leopold with his son Sonny
daughter in law Phyllis's two boys L
standing, Marshall in the p

Family photog

Donegal circa 1940 Philip and Phyllis his daughter in law

Left to right; Rose Coss, Leslie, Phyllis and Philip Leopold

Family photographs courtesy Leslie Leopold

Summer holidays Donegal circa 1940s Beryl Rolston and her cousin Gloria Gould
Family photograph

Belfast circa 1930s
Left to right; Mac Gould (Peggy Leopold's Husband), Rose Leopold, Sonny Leopold
Family photograph

Belfast circa 1950s

Beryl Rolston and her closest friend Gladys Duffin

Beryl Rolston, Sylvia Morrow, Gladys Duffin Photograph Metro
Photo Service Belfast

Peggy Leopold Fancy dress party
Dublin circa 1930s

Photograph Courtesy of Metro Photo
Service

Ireland circa 2013 World Tour researching family
Mervyn Silverstein (grandson of beautiful Dolly Leopold) and his wife Rae Stawski
whose parents survived Belsen Camp during the Holocaust

Photographs courtesy Mervyn and Rae Silverstein Australia

Sissy (Kathleen) Rolston circa 1930

Photographed by her brother Joseph Rolston

Carnboy Co.Fermanagh 1930s
Joseph Rolston (Tommy Rolston's eldest
brother) Engagement celebration portrait

Josie, as he became known, excelled in
architecture and photography. He too
would play his part in the War effort,
securing the job of clerk of works at
Castle Archdale during the
US Military presence
in N.Ireland.

Carnboy Co.Fermanagh 1930s

The house Josie built for him and his wife Margaret (Maggie) pictured in the doorway.
Every counter-top in the kitchen was built to suit Maggie's diminutive height.

Family photographs courtesy of Vincent Rolston

Carnboy Co.Fermanagh circa 1950s Hay-making
Left to right; Tommy and George Rolston with Gerry Connon

Carnboy Co.Fermanagh circa 1950s
Left to right; Jack, Beryl, Uncle George and Jim Rolston.
Front centre; cousin John Gallagher

Family photographs

Larne circa 1963 Always a doll to dress
Beryl and Roisin Connon, May Gallagher
(nee Rolston) tailoress, Geraldine Connon

Family photograph

Larne circa 1956 Beryl Rolston &
Gerry Connon Wedding

Left to right; Jim Rolston, Mary Connon,
Driver Gerry and Beryl Photograph courtesy
of Cedric Browne son of Mr Browne, a
highly accomplished local photographer as
it turns out who used to disappear to Belfast
every Christmas bearing gifts for a close
friend, Henri Solomon Two gentlemen who
understood the beauty of photography

Belfast circa 1953
Philip Leopold somewhat recovered from the losses of the War. Loving his extended family

Portrait Henri Solomon
Permission of use Malka Coler California USA

Larne 1956 Wedding Breakfast, Kings Arms Hotel
Bea Leopold Freeman and her niece Beryl Rolston Connon

Family photograph

y Connon 'First and Last Bar'
on Road, Larne circa 1955

ily photograph

CONNON BROTHERS
1950s

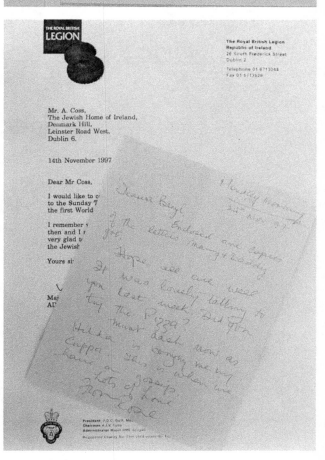

Invite to Medal
Presentation Dublin

The 'Legion d'Honneur'
presentation, Dublin
circa 2000

Millie & Albert Coss
with nephew Richard
Leopold who flew
in from Washington
Family photograph

Madam Helena Rubenstein
and Richard Leopold
circa 1960 New York USA
Photographer unknown

New Jersey USA circa 2001 left to right
Richard Leopold, Stephen Hylands, Geraldine Connon

Family photograph

Mexico 1980s
Guita Schyfter, granddaughter of Michael Lepar

Courtesy of Guita Schyfter Mexico City

Israel 2000 Collective imagery Masada
Joseph top of the steps in Bethlehem
Geraldine and David Mount of Olives
Geraldine at The Wailing Wall

Private photographs

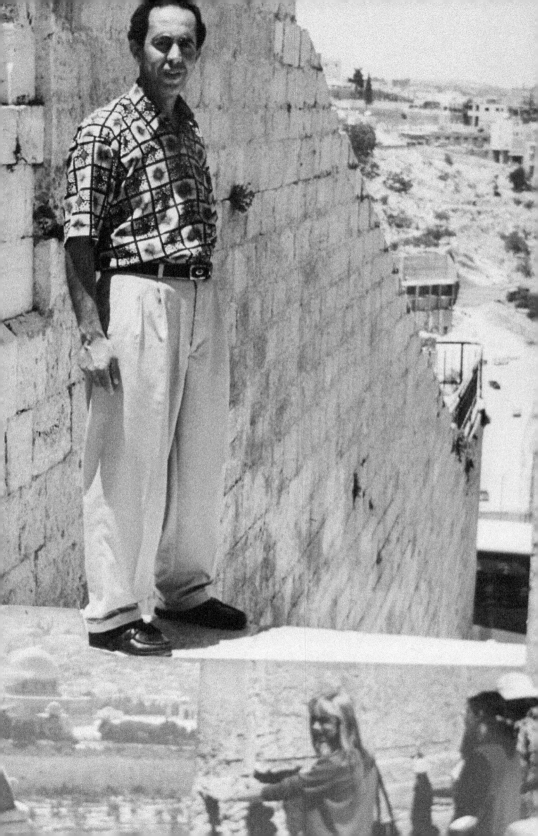

Carnboy Co.Fermanagh circa 1950s
Vincent Rolston and Brandy

Family photograph

THE ART OF TAILORIN

PARISIAN INSPIRED

Étoiles Collection

PREMIERED

CLANDEBOYE ESTATE

17TH AUGUST 2017

GERALDINE CONNON
MADE TO MEASURE

FACEBOOK: GERALDINE GONNON
WWW.GERALDINECONNON.COM

JOANNA, MAUREEN MARTIN MODELS
ACCESSORIES
VINTAGE DIOR BROACH 1961
JIMMY CHOO SHOES
HAND CROCHET GLOVES BY UNA LAGHLOAD

PHOTOGRAPHY
MITCHELL CAHOON
WWW.MITCHELLCAHOONPHOTOGRAPHY.CO.UK

Tatler photograph imagery Mitchell Cahoon photography

Clandeboye Estate, Camerata Music Festival
Ella, Maureen Martin Models, hair by Stephen Mc Cusker, makeup by Oonagh Boman
RoundThorn Sport Horses, Crumlin
Fly veil Olvossa

Photographer Mitchell Cahoon

Camerata Music Festival
Clandeboye Estate

Left to right; Maureen Martin,
Maureen Martin Models, Barry
Douglas classical Pianist and
founder of Camerata;
Geraldine Connon

Photographer Mitchell Cahoon

'Save the Children' Fashion Show Hillsborough Castle circa 2011 Left to right catwalk; Ella, Maureen Martin Models, Natalie Nwagbo freelance model London wearing GC Label Bespoke Gatsby Collection in wool silk and faux fur

Photograph courtesy Darren Kidd Press Eye

Ella (Maureen Martin Models)
on the catwalk wearing GC Label
Bespoke Irish tweed

Photograph courtesy
Darren Kidd Press eye

'Art in Linen' Book launch N.Ireland Linen Museum, Lisburn 2012 Left to right in focus; Isobel Tweed, Gerardine Mulvenna, Beryl Connon, Hannah Craig, Peter Heywood, Brian Mackey

Photograph courtesy Kelvin Boyes Press eye

Stormont Parliament Buildings 'For the love of Fashion' 2014 Backstage Left to right;
Amy Connon, Natalie Nwagbo London, Una Lashford, Gemma McAllister, Laura Cowan
Maureen Martin Models

Photograph courtesy Darren Kidd Press eye

Bespoke Silk taffeta Pin-stripe
Dress Suit GC Label

Photograph Joe McKay Larne

Bespoke Silk evening gown GC Label
Photograph Joe McKay Larne

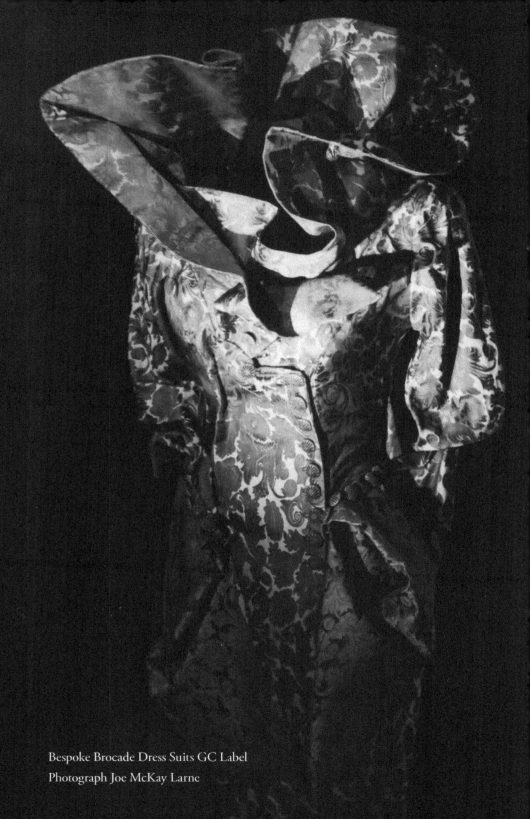

Bespoke Brocade Dress Suits GC Label

Photograph Joe McKay Larne

Bespoke Ball Gown, Velvet and Tulle with Flowers
GC Label Rebecca Maguire
Miss Ireland 2012

Photographer Mitchell Cahoon

Nachum Lepar Israel circa 1950s
Photograph courtesy Sarah Lubratski Israel

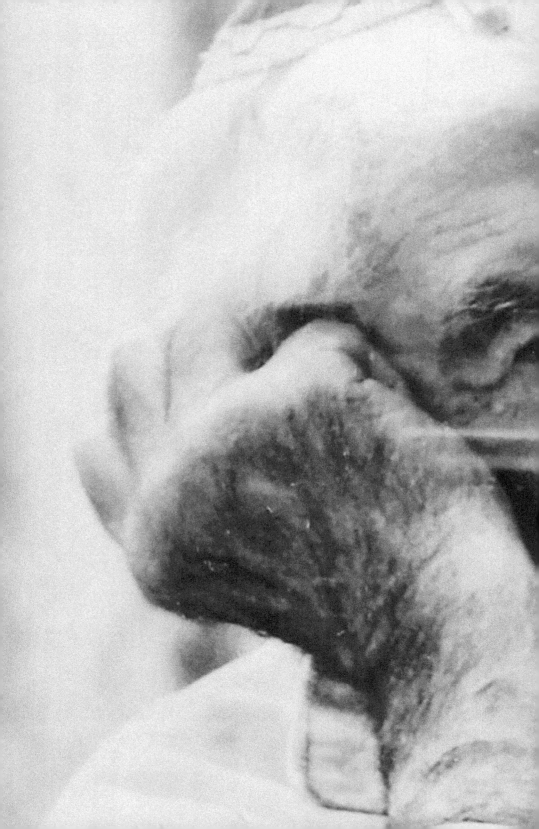

Nachum Lepar, Israel circa 1980s
Photograph courtesy Sarah Lubratski Israel

Sarah Lubratski Israel
circa 2020 daughter
of Nachum son of
Shmuel Lepar

Photograph courtesy
Sarah Lubratski Israel

Kriukai Lithuania circa 1920s

Barry and Bassa Lepar parents of
Alec Lepar Leopold Barry was a
brother of Philip Leopold

Photograph courtesy
Sarah Lubratski Israel

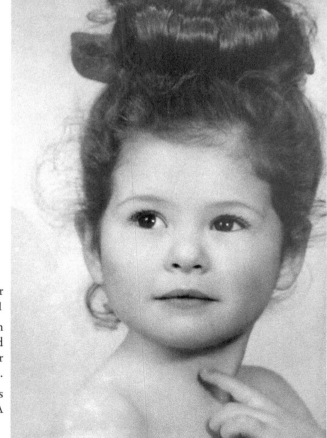

Shira Bliss photographed by her
grandfather Henri Solomon 1961

Miss Pears Competition London
earning them a fabulous second
place to the Queen's photographer
on this occasion.

Photograph courtesy of Shira Bliss
and Malka Coler California USA

Henri Solomon The artistic photographic genius
of his day.

Photographer to 'High Society' and media stars. A truly
gifted man with an eye for detail and elegance who so
easily captured poignant beauty in all of his subjects.

Philip Leopold's firm friend behind the camera lens.

Mr Solomon who disarmingly described himself
as "conceited" excelled in child portraiture, yet
photographed four generations of the same families many
times. He lived and breathed photography attending
at least forty conferences touring England, Ireland,
Scotland and the United States claiming to be the
oldest member of his profession in the British Isles as he
approached his 75th birthday. Three close friends were
Mr Browne of Larne, Mr A.R.Hogg of Belfast and Mr
John Brinkley of Glasgow. At one memorable winter
session of the Professional Photographer's Association
of Belfast held at Henri s' studio in Donegall Place, the
topic was that of the importance of Child photography.
The great point was the treatment of the child in the
studio and all the tactics used in capturing the perfect
expression. Mr Brinkley, who would not allow more
than one person to accompany the child to the studio,
claimed that the one thing that made the camera capable
of artistic expression was the ideals of the man who
worked it. He would put it that the love of children was
God given and without that love no man could be a
successful photographer of children.The modern studio
now 1966 was equipped with toys and things to interest
them in their play- sea-side backgrounds, sand,spades and
pails- but of more importance nowadays was simplicity,
expression, naturalness and lighting. The chat played
out and it was agreed success attended the photographer
who became a child himself for the time being. Humour
followed by laughter and maybe another phrase was
coined when it was claimed that when all tactics failed
with one little boy and finally he was asked what he liked
best for his dinner.

An immediate reply, "sausages," caused him to assume
the right expression and he was snapped in a flash.

Henri, when he photographed the Leopold girls at the
beginning of his career, already had that innate sense and
gift of vision. He found their depth of soul.

Photograph courtesy of Malka Coler and Shira Bliss
California USA

Letter to Neska from Geraldine, her granddaughter

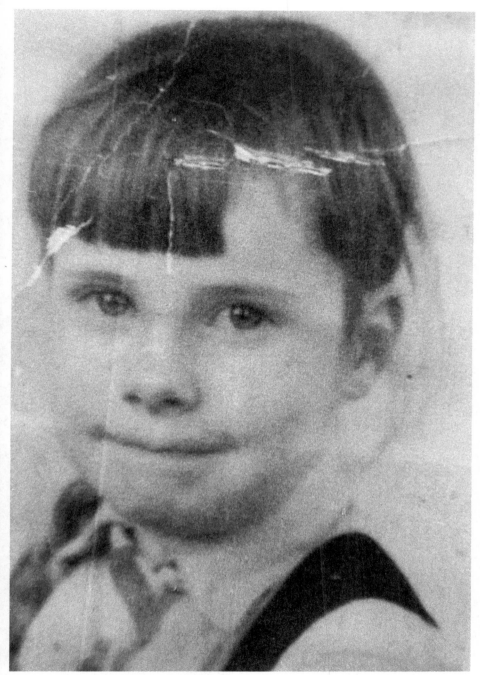

St. Marys Primary School Larne circa 1964
"Well, I hope you are all sassisfied now"
Geraldine Connon Childhood favourite quote

Photograph Mr Browne Larne

"That's a wrap"
Geraldine Connon Back Stage Hillsborough 'Save the Children Show' 2011
Photographer Darren Kidd courtesy of Press eye

Silk and Steel

Photographer Michael McKay

Model; Alannah

Location; The interim wasteland of Harland and Wolff shipyard
from those glory days before redevelopment.

Ticket Image for GC 21 year Celebratory Fashion Show
Europa Hotel Belfast for Children in Need

THE WRITERS

Divide and conquer the war cry of Empires, the decree of rulers and the yell of dictators. It is like a constant sickening, wearisome and pathetic echo in the background of millions of lives worldwide somewhere and at some point. in time, forever and a day.

Stop, in God Almighty's name, stop.

This is our very human story, set 130 years apart. Beginning in the 1870s Western Ukraine when the Slavic countries were under the rule of the Tsars of the Russian Empire and finishing a fait accompli 11th March 2022 in Northern Ireland.

Dedicated with love to
Beryl and Gerry Connon.

Lightning Source UK Ltd.
Milton Keynes UK
UKHW012103140622
404434UK00001B/46